The Ultimate Guitar Songbook

ISBN 0-7935-8554-6

HAL•LEONARD® CORPORATION

7777 W. BLUEMOUND RD. P.O. BOX 13819 MILWAUKEE, WI 53213

Visit Hal Leonard Online at
www.halleonard.com

The Ultimate Guitar Songbook

Guitar Recorded Versions

4 Babe, I'm Gonna Leave You

18 Brown Eyed Girl

25 Dust in the Wind

28 Here Comes the Sun

33 Love Struck Baby

43 No Particular Place to Go

50 Paranoid

54 You Really Got Me

Easy Guitar with Notes and TAB

58 The Addams Family Theme

59 Amazing Grace

62 Auld Lang Syne

66 The Best of My Love

60 Blue Suede Shoes

70 Boot Scootin' Boogie

63 Change the World

74 Chattahoochee

80 Counting Blue Cars

84 Danny Boy (Londonderry Air)

86 Don't Get Around Much Anymore

77 Don't Speak

88 El Shaddai

94 Free Bird

91 Great Balls of Fire

98 Greensleeves

99 Mission: Impossible Theme

100 The Munster's Theme

102 My One and Only Love

104 Only Wanna Be With You

108 Rock Around the Clock

110 Sweet Home Chicago

112 Vision of Love

117 Wonderwall

122 Yesterday

124 You Were Meant for Me

127 Your Song

Easy Guitar

130 Achy Breaky Heart (Don't Tell My Heart)

132 All My Loving

134 Are You Sleeping

138 Ave Maria

136 Back in the U.S.S.R.

139 Beauty and the Beast

140 Born to Be Wild

142 The Boys Are Back in Town

144 Crazy

145 Edelweiss

146 Friends in Low Places

148 Have I Told You Lately

150 He's Got the Whole World in His Hands

134 Hello, Dolly!

151	Home on the Range
150	House of the Rising Sun
157	Jingle Bells
152	Layla
154	Let It Be
155	Love Me Do
158	Maggie May
160	Mercury Blues
162	My Generation
163	My Girl
164	O Little Town of Bethleham
165	Rocky Mountain Way
166	Roxanne
168	Some Enchanted Evening
170	The Sound of Music
172	The Star Spangled Banner
174	Takin' Care of Business
177	T-R-O-U-B-L-E
176	We Will Rock You
180	When the Saints Go Marching In
181	Wild Thing
184	Yankee Doodle
182	You Needed Me

Chord Melody Guitar

185	All the Things You Are
188	The Christmas Song (Chestnuts Roasting on an Open Fire)
192	Misty
196	Stella by Starlight

Classical Guitar

201	Bianco Fiore
200	Estudio (Aguado)
202	Estudio #2 (Sor)
204	Lagrima
199	Minuet
206	Minuet
207	Pavane

Fingerstyle Guitar

208	Bury Me Not on the Lone Prairie
212	My Funny Valentine
210	Scarborough Fair
215	Shenandoah
216	Tears in Heaven
219	A Whole New World (Aladdin's Theme)

Guitar Riffs

222	All Day and All of the Night
222	All Right Now
223	Crazy Train
223	Cult of Personality
224	Day Tripper
224	Deuce
225	I Feel Fine
225	I'll Stick Around
226	I'm Your Hoochie Coochie Man
226	Iron Man
227	Message in a Bottle
227	Money
228	More Than a Feeling
228	Name
229	Oh, Pretty Woman
229	Paperback Writer
230	Smoke on the Water
230	Start Me Up
231	Substitute
231	Sunshine of Your Love
232	Sweet Home Alabama
232	Walk This Way

233	**Strum and Pick Patterns**
234	**Guitar Notation Legend**

Babe, I'm Gonna Leave You

Words and Music by Anne Bredon, Jimmy Page and Robert Plant

na leave ____ you. _____ I'll _____

____ leave you _ when _ the sum-mer-time, _____ leave you when the ___ sum - mer comes

a - roll - in,' leave __ you when ___ the sum - mer __ comes _

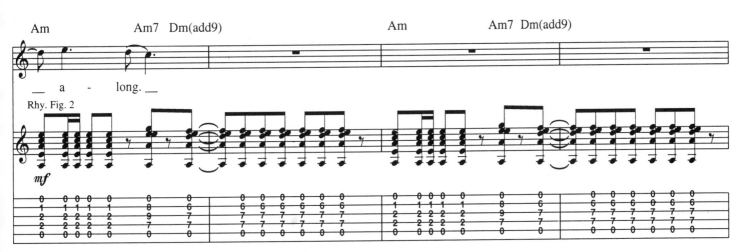

__ a - long. __

Rhy. Fig. 2

mf

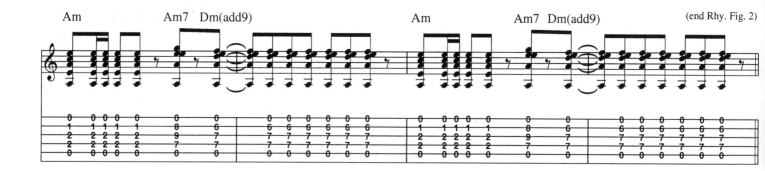

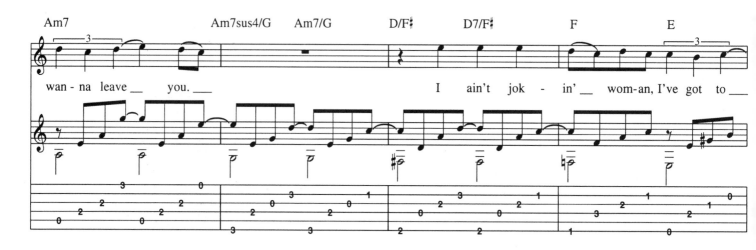

I could hear it call - in' me, ____ I said don't you hear it call -in' me the way it

used to do? ____ Oh. _____

I know,_____ I know,___ I know I nev-er, nev-er, nev-er, nev-er, nev-er gon-na

(Gtr. 2 out)

leave you babe,_ but I got-ta go a-way from this place._

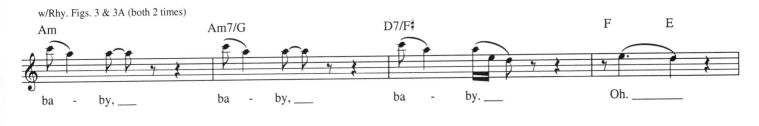

It was real - ly,   real - ly good. ___

You made   me hap-py ev-'ry __ sin- gle

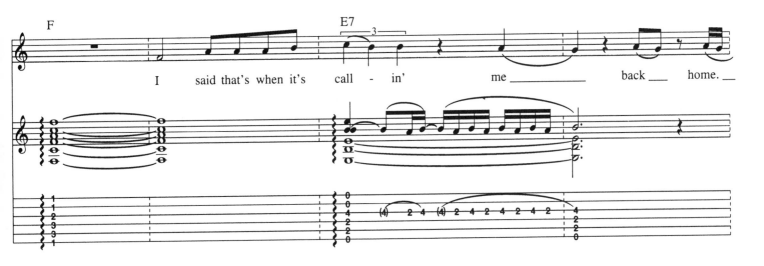

I said that's when it's call - in' me _____ back ___ home. __

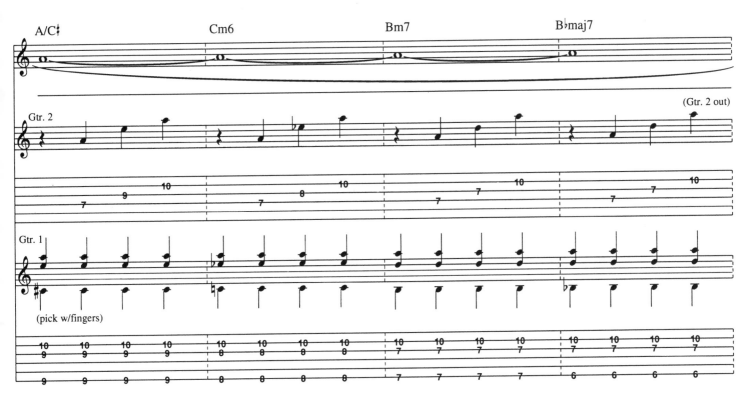

(pick w/fingers)

Brown Eyed Girl

Words and Music by Van Morrison

G C D7 Em

21 34   32 1   213   23

Intro
Moderately Fast Rock ♩ = 144

N.C.(G) (C) (G) 1. (D)

Gtr. 1 (elec.)

mf

w/ clean tone
w/ pick & fingers

2.

(D)

Verse
G C G

Gtr. 2
(acous.)

mf

Rhy. Fig. 1

Hey, where did we go ___ days _ when the rains _

Gtr. 1

let ring

Gtr. 2: w/ Rhy. Fig. 1, 3 times

D7 G C

End Rhy. Fig. 1

___ came? ___

Down _ in the hol - low, _

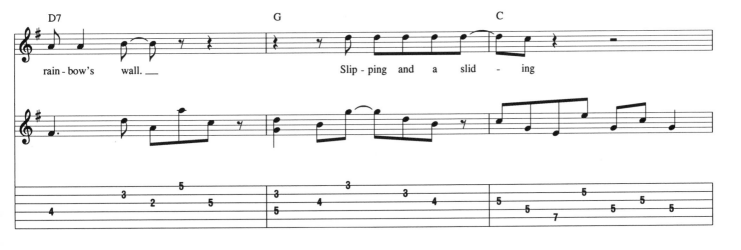

Chorus

Gtr. 2: w/ Rhy. Fig. 1, 2 times

Sha, la, la, la, la, la, la, la, la, la, la, te, da.

Just like that. Sha, la, la, la, la, la, la, la,

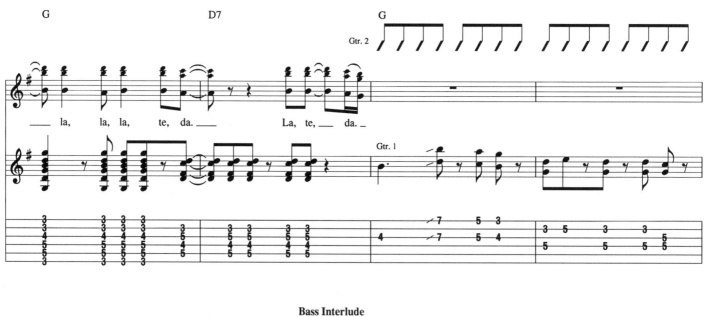

la, la, la, te, da. La, te, da.

Bass Interlude

Gtrs. 1 & 2 tacet

N.C.(G)　　　(C)　　　(G)　　　(D7)

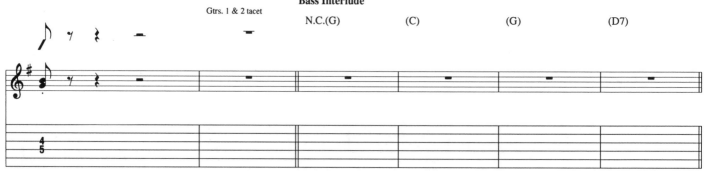

22

Verse

Gtr. 2: w/ Rhy. Fig. 1, 4 times

3. So hard to find ____ my way now ____ that I'm all ____ on my ____ own. ____

I saw you just ____ the oth-er day; ____ my, ____ how you have grown. ____

Cast ____ my mem-'ry back ____ there, Lord. Some - times I'm o -

ver - come think - in' 'bout ____ it. Laugh-ing and a run - ning, hey, ____ hey, ____

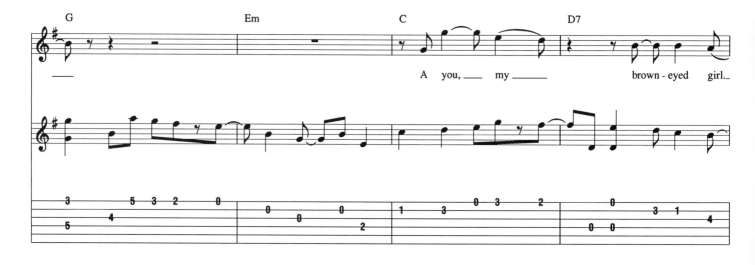

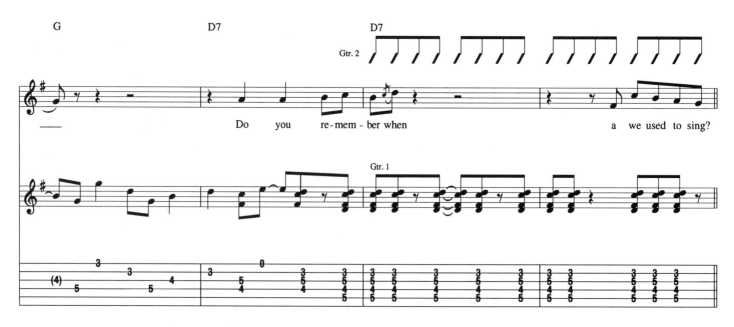

Chorus

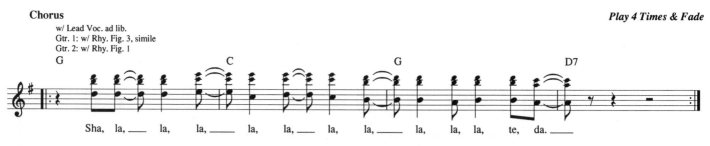

Dust in the Wind

Words and Music by Kerry Livgren

All my dreams _____ pass be-fore_ my eyes,_ a cu - ri -
All we do _____ and crum-bles to _ the ground though we re -
slips a - way _____ and all your mon - ey won't _ an - oth - er

Chorus   *To Coda* ⊕

os - i - ty. _
fuse to see. _ }
min - ute buy. _

Dust   in   the   wind

All they are _ is   dust   in _ the _ wind.
    (we)

wind. _____

Oh,   ho,   ho.

Instrumental Bridge

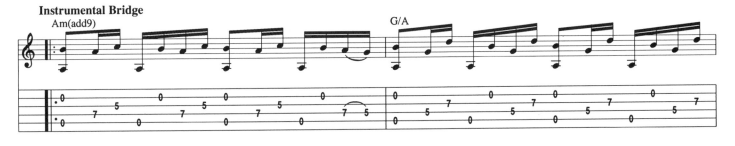

D.C. al Coda

✦ *Coda*

All we are ___ is dust in ___ the wind. ___
(All we are ___ is dust in ___ the

Dust _____ in ___ the wind.
wind. _____ Ev - 'ry-thing _ is dust in ___ the

Ev - 'ry-thing _ is dust in ___ the
wind.)

Outro

Play 4 Times and Fade

wind.

The ____ wind. _

ad lib. voc. on repeat

Here Comes The Sun

Words and Music by George Harrison

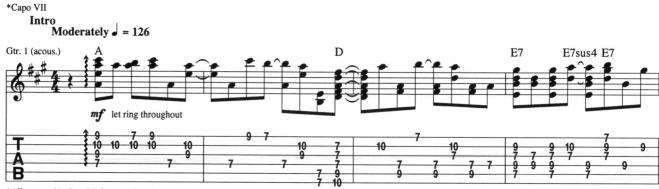

*Capo VII

Intro

Moderately ♩ = 126

Gtr. 1 (acous.)

mf let ring throughout

*All notes tabbed on 7th fret are played as open strings

Chorus

Here comes _ the sun, ____ doo 'n' doo doo. Here comes _ the sun _

_ 'n' I __ say _ it's al - right.

Verse

1. Lit-tle dar-lin', it's __ been __ a __ long, __ cold, __ lone - ly win - ter.

Lit-tle dar-lin', it __ feels __ like __ years __ since it's __ been __ here. __

Chorus

Here comes_ the sun, __ doo 'n' doo doo. Here _ comes_ the sun __ 'n' I __ say

it's al - right.

Verse

2. Lit-tle dar-lin', the smiles _ re-turn - ing to _ their fac - es.

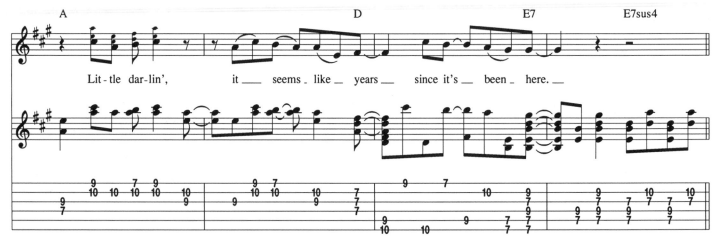

Lit-tle dar-lin', it _ seems _ like _ years _ since it's _ been _ here. _

% Chorus

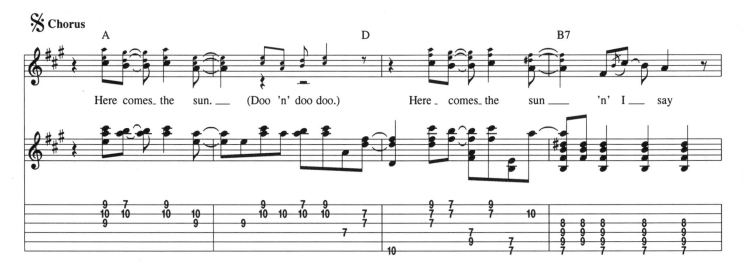

Here comes_ the sun. _ (Doo 'n' doo doo.) Here _ comes_ the sun _ 'n' I _ say

To Coda ⊕

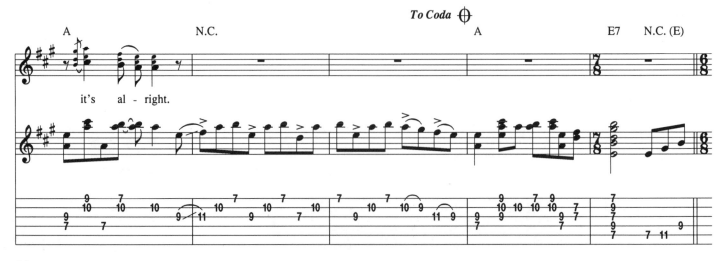

it's al - right.

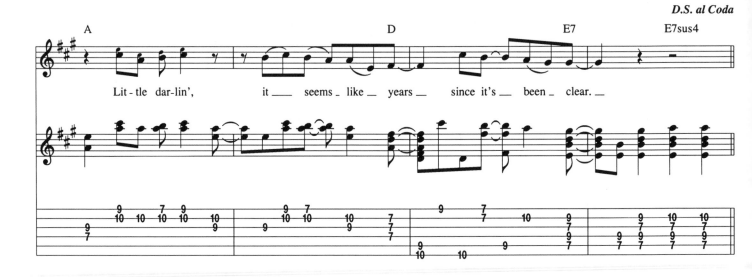

Lit - tle dar-lin', it ___ seems ___ like ___ years ___ since it's ___ been ___ clear. ___

 Coda

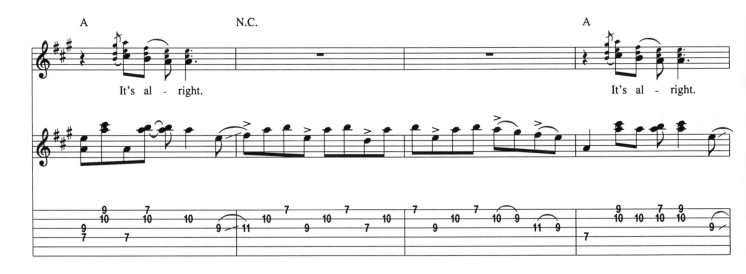

Here comes ___ the sun. ___ (Doo 'n' doo doo.) Here comes ___ the sun. ___

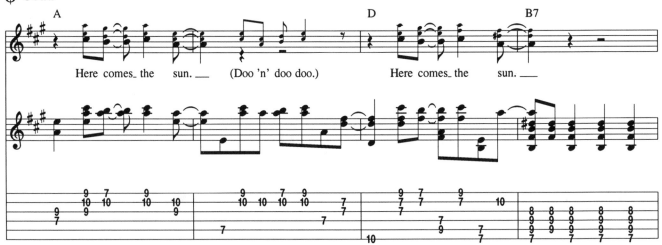

It's al - right. It's al - right.

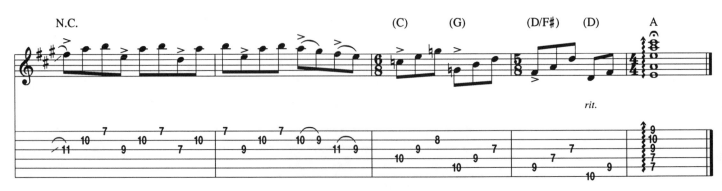

Love Struck Baby

Words and Music by Stevie Ray Vaughan

* 6 string bass arr. for gtr.

** Gtr. 2 played one octave higher
than gtr. part, resulting in same pitch.

*** Chord symbols reflect overall harmony.

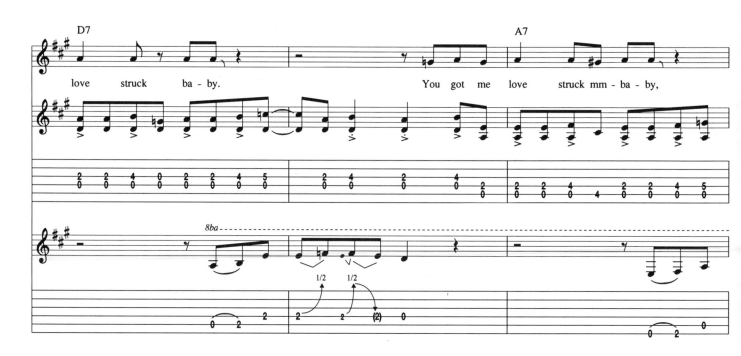

love struck ba - by. You got me love struck mm - ba - by,

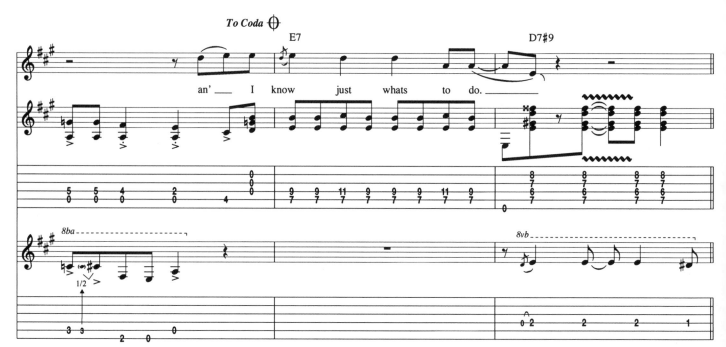

To Coda ⊕

an' ___ I know just whats to do. ___

Bass Solo

Gtr. 2

Gtr. 1

Barely audible next 9 meas.

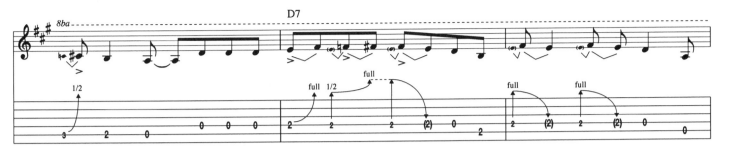

Guitar Solo (S.R.V.)

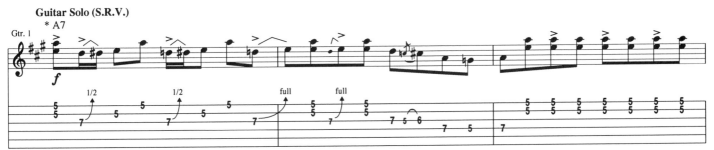

* Chord symbols reflect overall harmony.

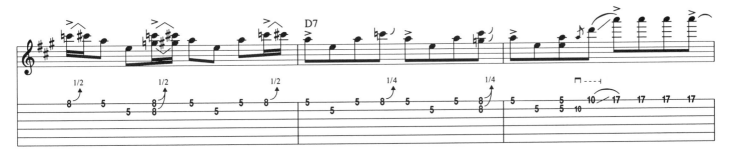

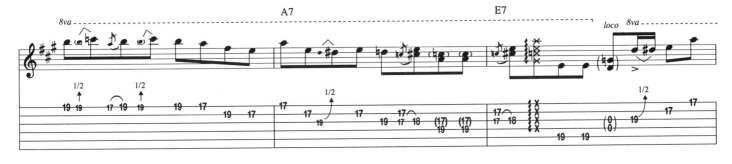

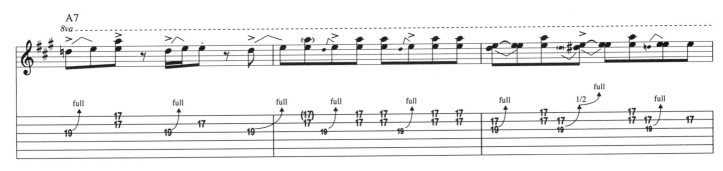

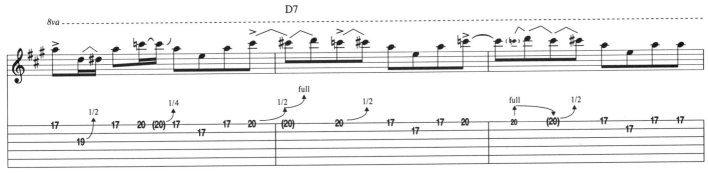

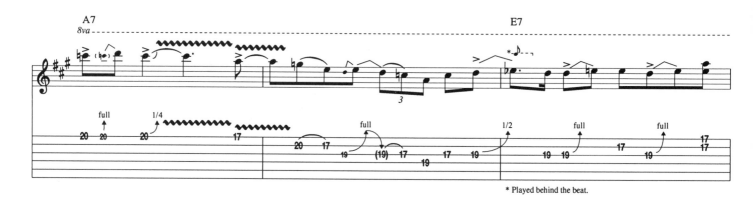

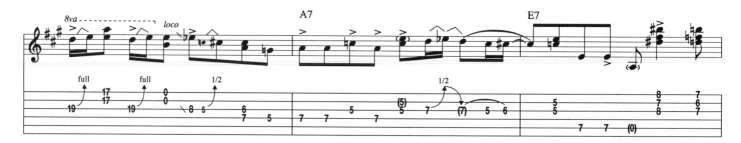

* Played behind the beat.

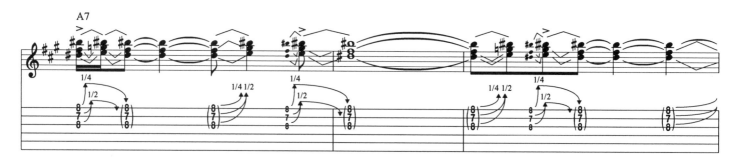

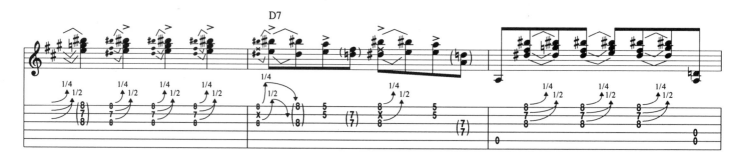

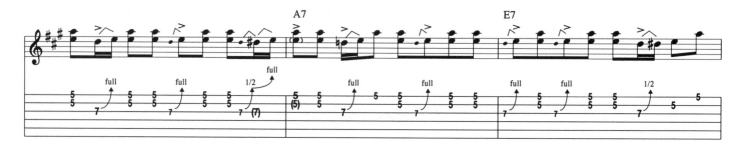

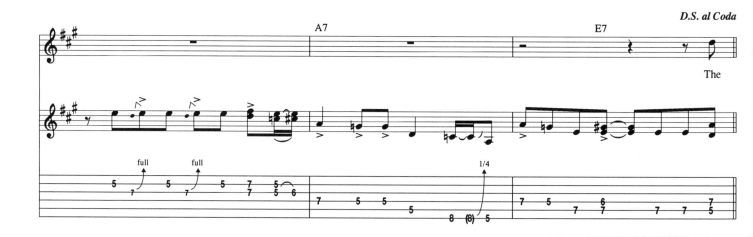

The

⊕ Coda

know just what to do. ____

Ow!

Freely

No Particular Place to Go

Words and Music by Chuck Berry

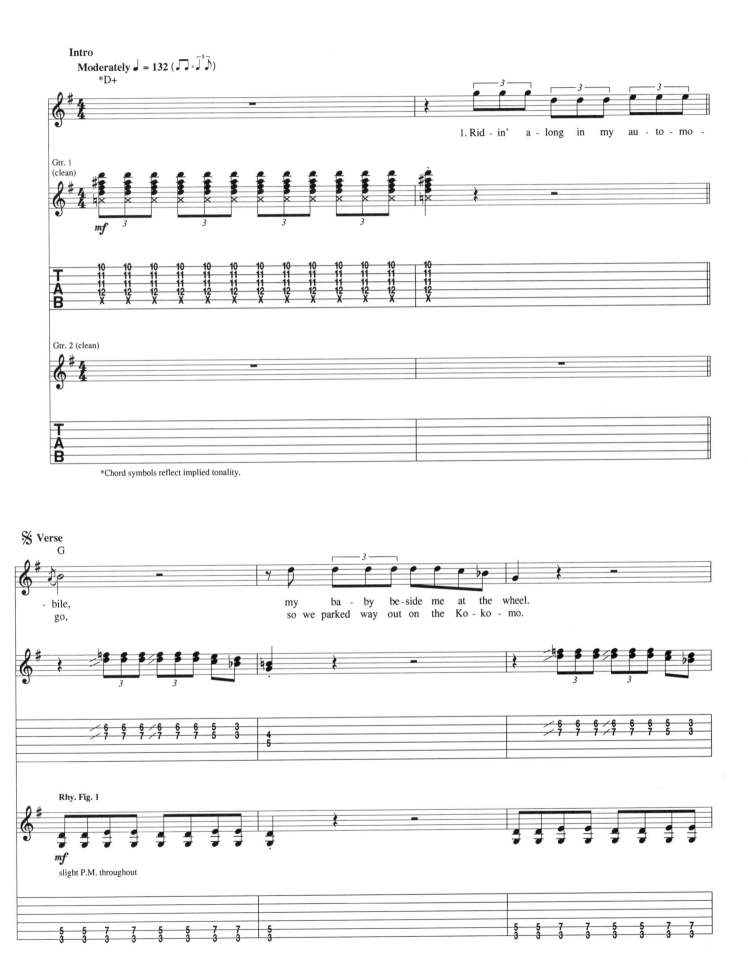

*Chord symbols reflect implied tonality.

with no   par - tic - u - lar place to   go
I could - n't un - fas - ten her safe - ty   belt.

2. Rid - in' a - long in my au - to - mo -
4. Rid - in' a - long in my cal - a - boose, _

End Rhy. Fig. 1

Verse

Gtr. 2: w/ Rhy. Fig. 1

G

bile,
still   try - in' to   get _ her belt   a - loose.

I's   anx - ious to tell her the way   I   feel.

Gtr. 1

C

So I told her soft - ly and sin - cere,
All _ the way home I held a grudge

and she leaned and whis - pered in   my
for the safe - ty belt that would - n't budge. _

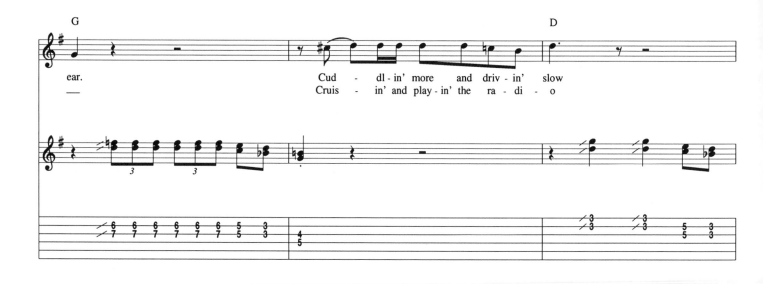

ear.

Cud - dl-in' more and driv - in' slow
Cruis - in' and play - in' the ra - di - o

To Coda

with no par - tic - u - lar place to go.
with no par - tic - u - lar place to

Guitar Solo

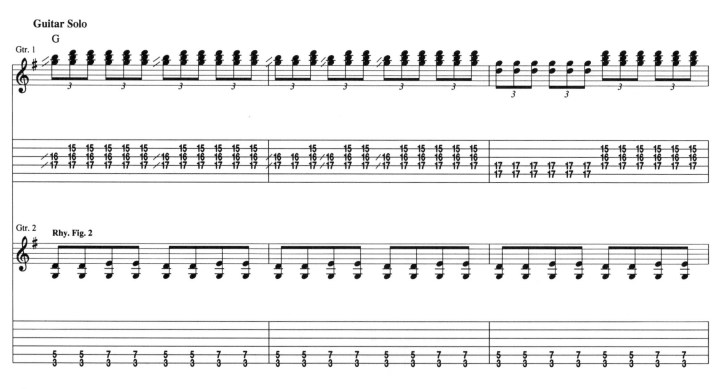

Gtr. 1
G

Gtr. 2
Rhy. Fig. 2

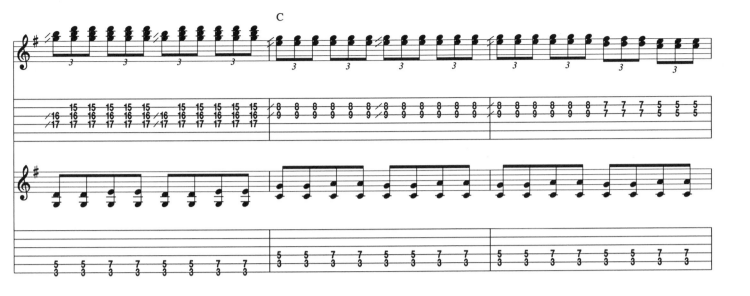

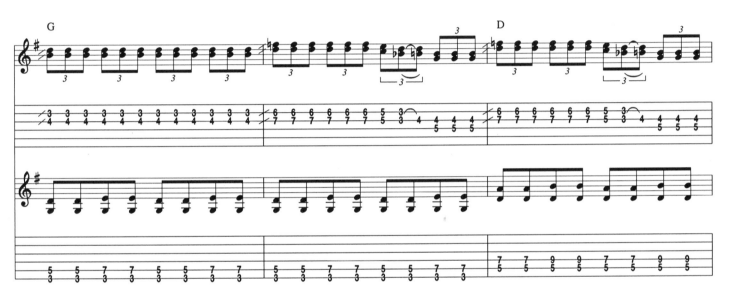

D.S. al Coda

3. No par - tic - u - lar place to

End Rhy. Fig. 2

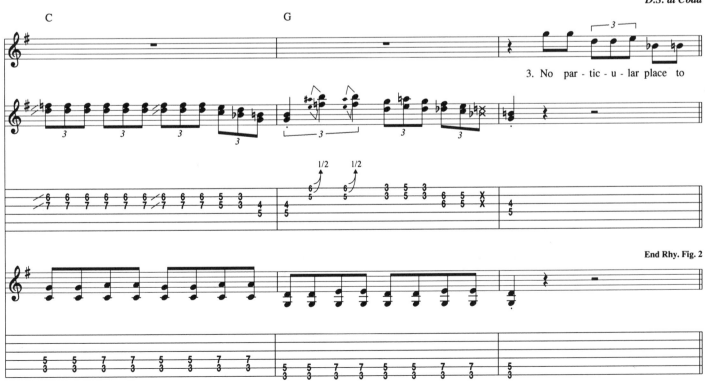

$\oplus$ *Coda*

Outro-Guitar Solo
Gtr. 2 w/ Rhy. Fig. 2

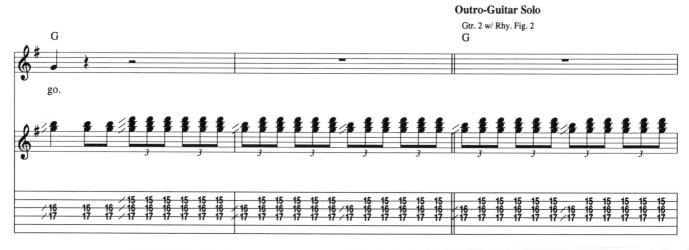

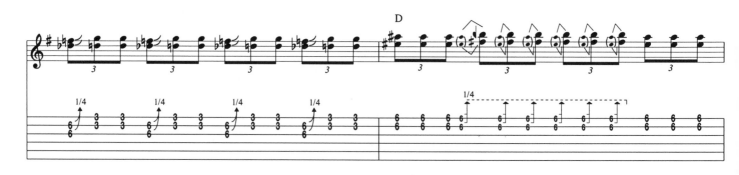

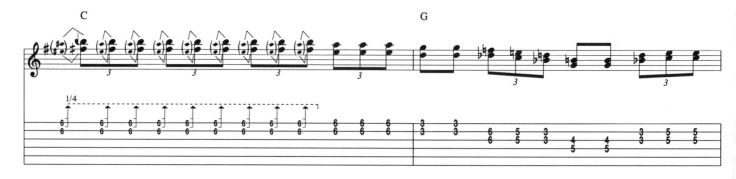

Gtr. 2: w/ Rhy. Fig. 2, 1st 10 meas.

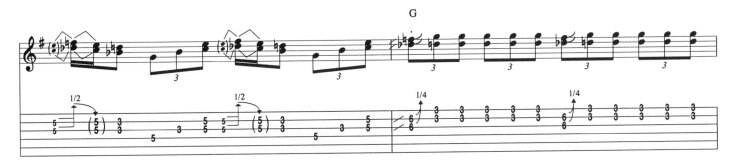

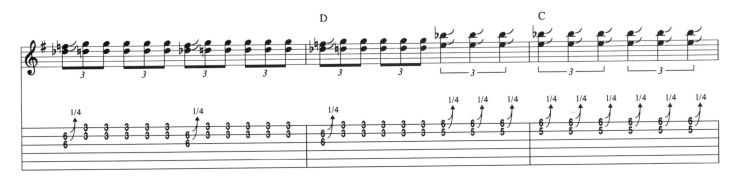

Paranoid

Words and Music by Anthony Iommi, John Osbourne, William Ward and Terence Butler

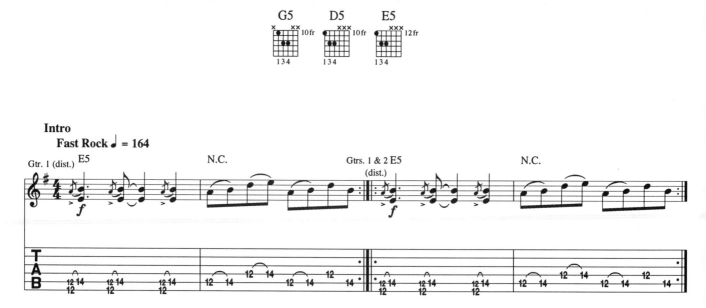

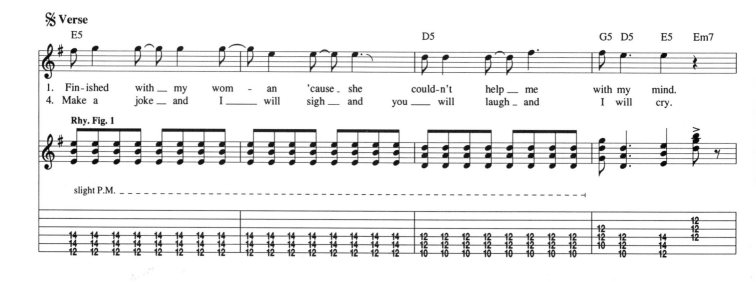

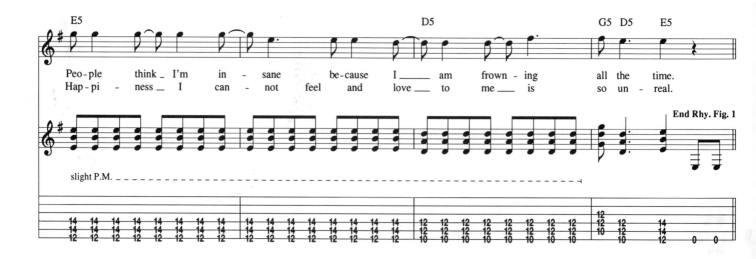

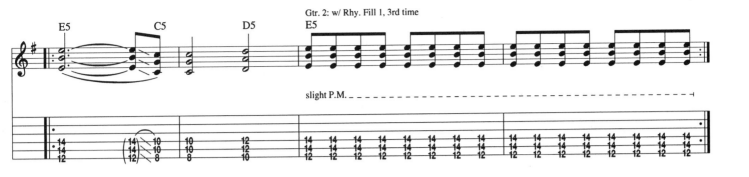

Verse

2. All day long ___ I think ___ of things ___ but noth-ing seems ___ to sat - is - fy.
5. And so as ___ you hear ___ these words ___ tell-ing you now ___ of ___ my state.

Think I'll lose ___ my mind ___ if I ___ don't find ___ some - thing ___ to pass it by.
I tell you ___ to en - joy life, ___ I wish ___ I could ___ but it's too late.

Bridge

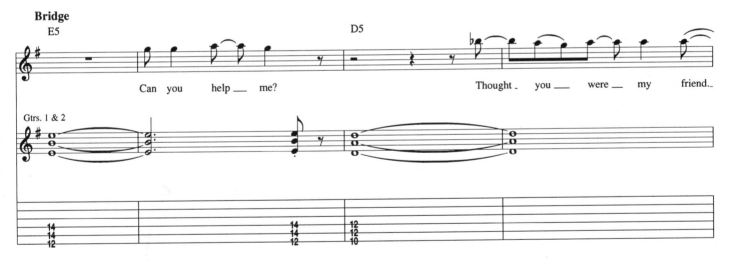

Can you help ___ me?

Thought ___ you ___ were ___ my friend. ___

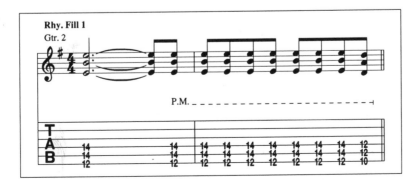

Whoa, _____ yeah! —

Interlude

slight P.M. -

Verse

Gtrs. 1 & 2: w/ Rhy. Fig. 1

3. I need some - one to ____ show me ___ the things ___ in life ___ that I can't find.

I can't see ___ the things ___ that make ___ true hap - pi - ness, ___ I must be blind.

Guitar Solo

Gtr. 2: w/ Rhy. Fig. 1, 1st 4 meas., 4 times

*Gtr. 1

1 1/2

*With heavily distorted ring modulation effect in right channel.

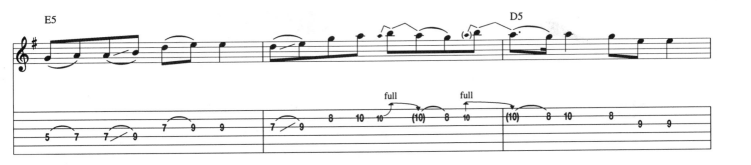

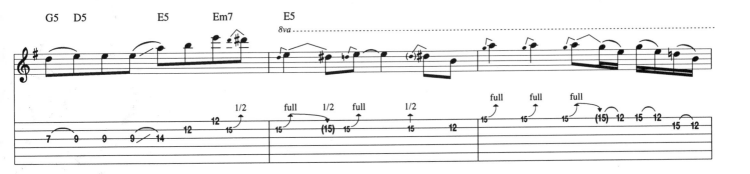

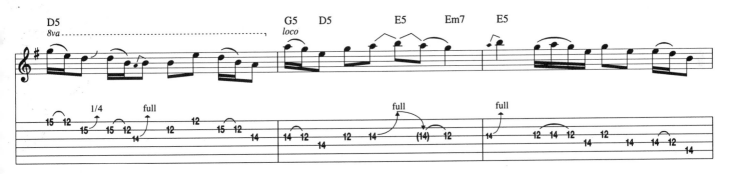

Interlude

D.S. al Coda

Gtrs. 1 & 2: w/ Rhy. Fig. 1,
1st 4 meas., 2 times

Coda

Outro

Gtrs. 1 & 2: w/ Rhy. Fig. 1, 1st 7 meas.

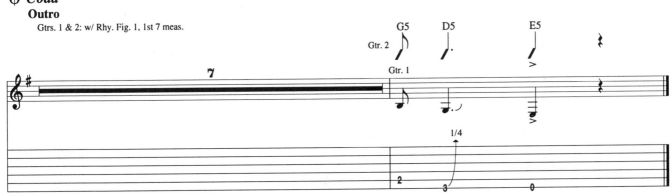

You Really Got Me

Words and Music by Ray Davies

so I can't sleep at night. ___
so I can't sleep at night. ___

Yeah,
(Yeah, _____

you real-ly

got me now, you got me so I don't know what I'm do-in', ___ ah.

Oh

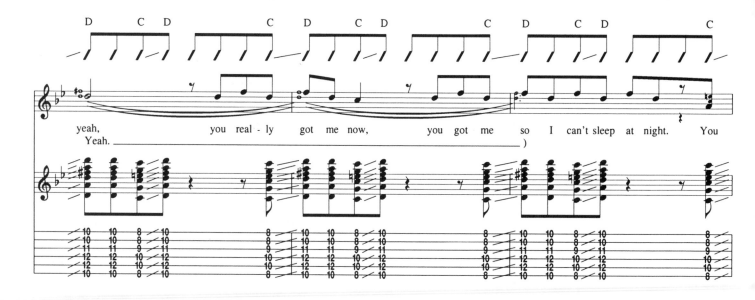

yeah, you real-ly got me now, you got me so I can't sleep at night. You
Yeah. _____)

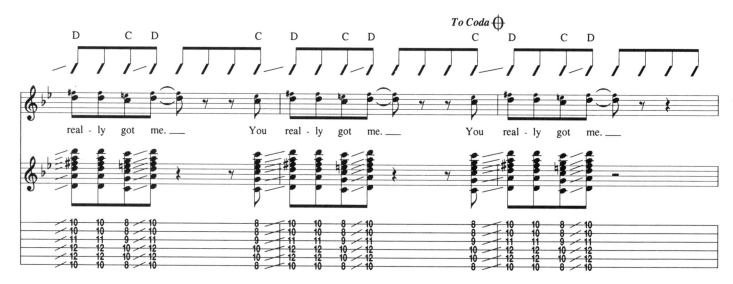

To Coda ✛

real-ly got me. ___ You real-ly got me. ___ You real-ly got me. ___

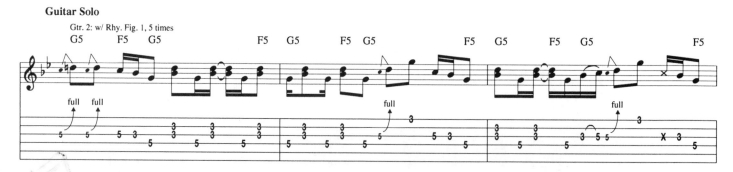

1.
C

2.
C

Oh, Lord. ___

full full full full full full 1/2

Guitar Solo
Gtr. 2: w/ Rhy. Fig. 1, 5 times

G5   F5   G5   F5   G5   F5   G5   F5   G5   F5   G5   F5

full full   full   full

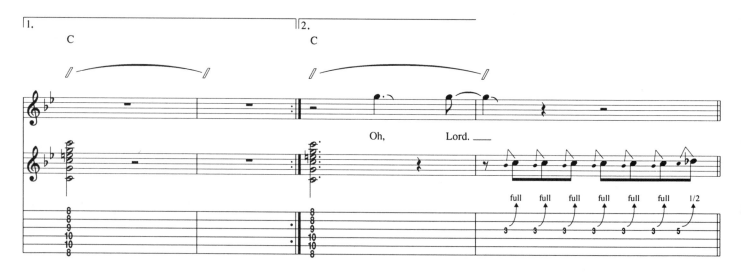

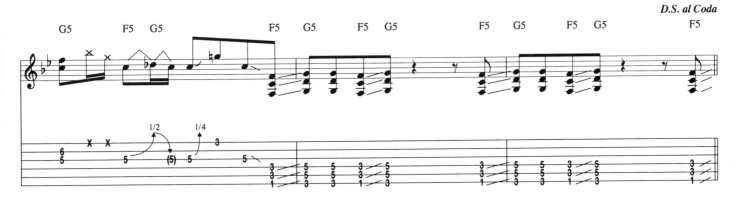

The Addams Family Theme

Music and Lyrics by Vic Mizzy

Strum Pattern: 3
Pick Pattern: 3

1. They're creep - y and they're kook - y, my - ster - i - ous and spook - y, they're
2., 3. *See Additional Lyrics*

al - to-geth - er ook - y, the Ad - dams fam - i - ly. 2. Their Ad - dams fam - i - ly.

Ad - dams fam - i - ly.

Additional Lyrics

2. Their house is a museum,
   Where people come to see 'em.
   They really are a screeum,
   The Addams family.

3. So get a witches shawl on,
   A broom stick you can crawl on,
   We're gonna pay a call on
   The Addams family.

Amazing Grace

Words by John Newton
Music by Virginia Harmony

Strum Pattern: 7
Pick Pattern: 7

Additional Lyrics

2. 'Twas grace that taught my heart to fear,
And grace my fears relieved.
How precious did that grace appear
The hour I first believed.

3. Through many dangers, toils and snares,
I have already come.
'Tis grace has brought me safe thus far,
And grace will lead me home.

4. The Lord has promised good to me,
His word my hope secures.
He will my shield and portion be
As long as life endures.

5. And when this flesh and heart shall fail,
And mortal life shall cease.
I shall possess within the veil
A life of joy and peace.

6. When we've been there ten thousand years,
Bright shining as the sun.
We've no less days to sing God's praise
Than when we first begun.

Blue Suede Shoes

Words and Music by Carl Lee Perkins

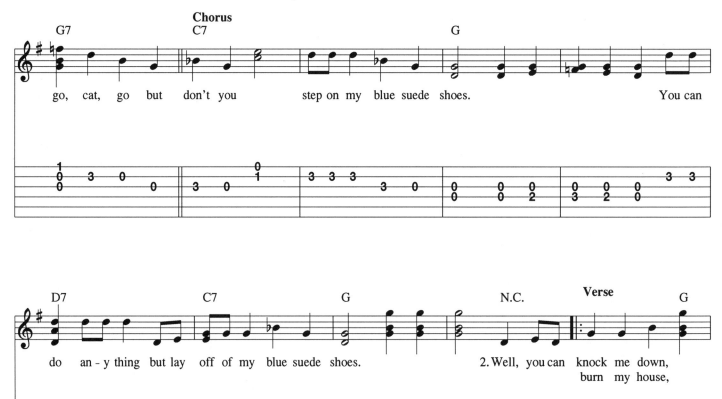

Strum Pattern: 2, 3
Pick Pattern: 3, 4

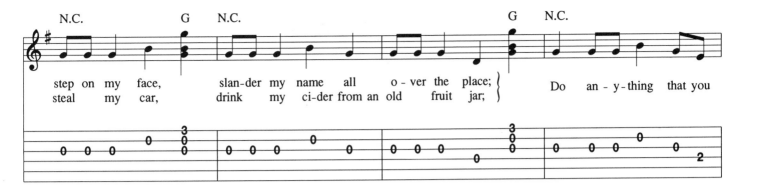

step on my face, slan-der my name all o-ver the place; Do an-y-thing that you
steal my car, drink my ci-der from an old fruit jar;

Chorus

want to do but uh-huh, hon-ey, lay off of my shoes. Now don't you

step on my blue suede shoes. You can do an-y-thing but lay

off of my blue suede shoes. 3. You can shoes.

Auld Lang Syne

Words by Robert Burns
Traditional Scottish Melody

Strum Pattern: 3
Pick Pattern: 3

Change the World

featured on the Motion Picture Soundtrack PHENOMENON

Words and Music by Gordon Kennedy, Tommy Sims and Wayne Kirkpatrick

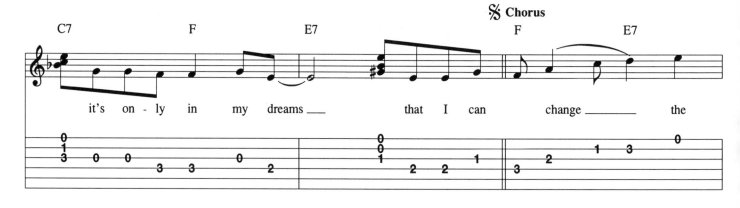

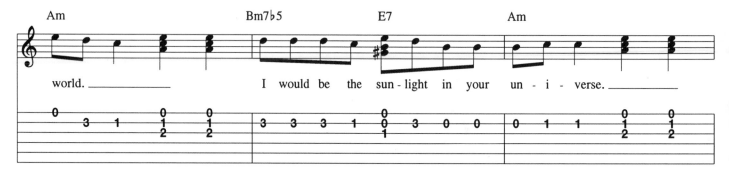

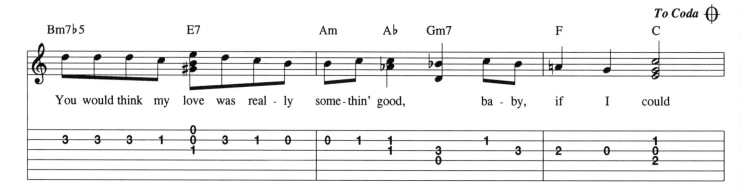

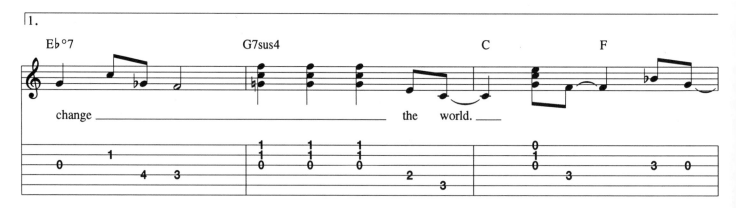

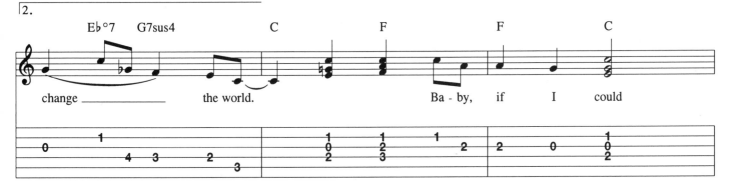

change _____ the world. Ba - by, if I could

change _____ the world. ___ I could

D.S. al Coda

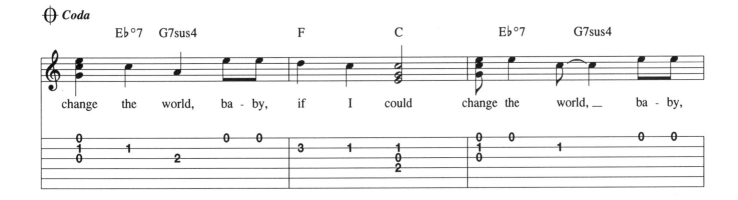

change the world, ba - by, if I could change the world, __ ba - by,

Coda

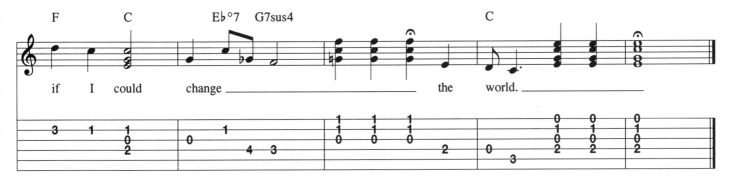

if I could change _____ the world. ____

Additional Lyrics

2. If I could be king
   Even for a day,
   I'd take you as my queen,
   I'd have it no other way.
   And our love would rule
   In this kingdom that we had made
   Till then I'll be a fool,
   Wishin' for the day...

The Best of My Love

Words and Music by John David Souther, Don Henley and Glenn Frey

Cmaj7add2   C   Fmaj7#11   Fmaj7   Cmaj7   F

Em7   Dm7   G   G7   G6   Fm

Strum Pattern: 1, 2
Pick Pattern: 2, 3

Intro
Moderately Slow

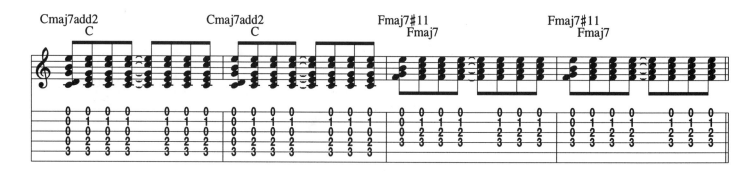

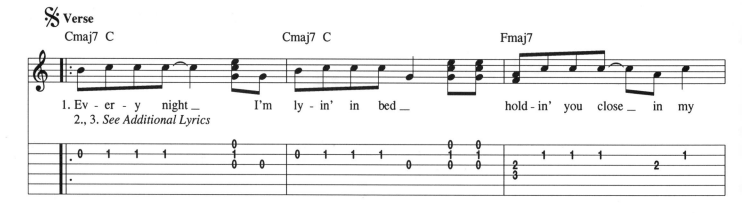

Verse

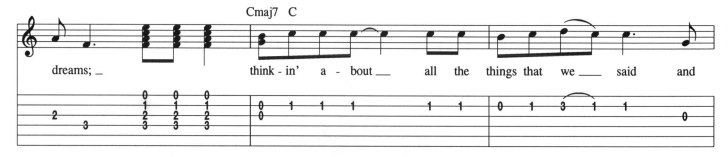

1. Ev-er-y night _ I'm ly-in' in bed _ hold-in' you close _ in my
2., 3. *See Additional Lyrics*

dreams; _ think-in' a-bout _ all the things that we _ said and

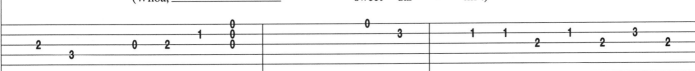

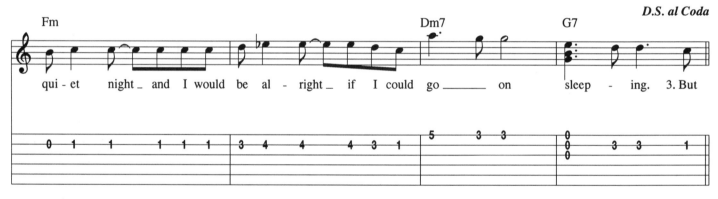

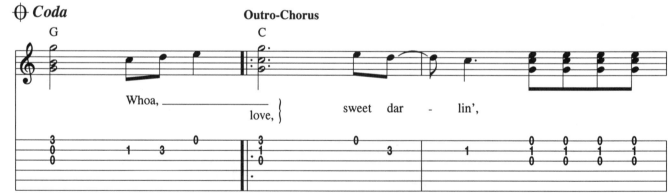

- lin', you get the best of my love, the best of my ___ love. ___ Sweet dar - lin', ev - 'ry night an' day, ___ you get the best of my

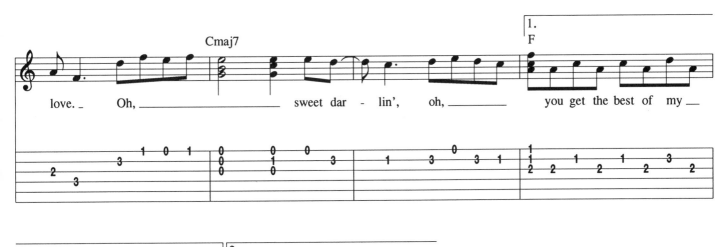

love. _ Oh, ___ sweet dar - lin', oh, ___ you get the best of my ___ love, the best of my

you get the best of my ___ love, the best of my love.

Additional Lyrics

2. Beautiful faces an' loud empty places, look at the way we live;
Wastin' our time on cheap talk and wine, left us so little to give.
That same old crowd was like a cold dark cloud that we could never rise above.
But here in my heart I give you the best of my love.

3. But ev'ry morning I wake up and worry what's gonna happen today.
You see it your way and I see it mine but we both see it slippin' away.
You know we always had each other, baby, I guess that wasn't enough;
Oh, oh, but here in my heart I give you the best of my love.

Boot Scootin' Boogie

Words and Music by Ronnie Dunn

Strum Pattern: 3, 4

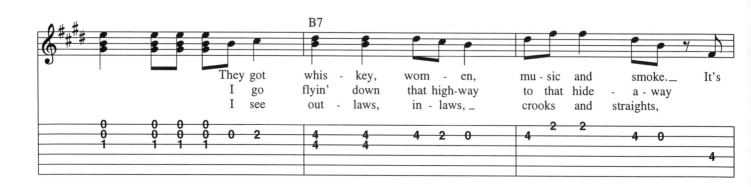

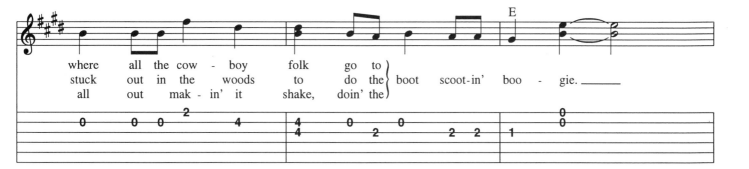

where all the cow - boy folk go to
stuck out in the woods to do the boot scoot-in' boo - gie. _____
all out mak - in' it shake, doin' the

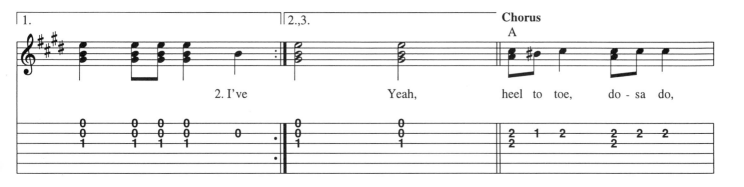

1.			2.,3.	**Chorus** A

2. I've Yeah, heel to toe, do - sa do,

E

come on ba - by, let's go boot scoot-in'! _ Whoa,

A

Cad - il - lac, Black - jack, ba - by meet me out back. We're gon - na

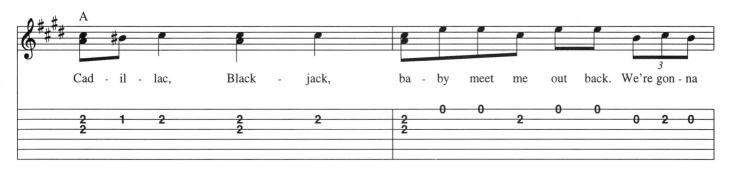

E   B7

boo - gie. Oh, get down, turn a - round,

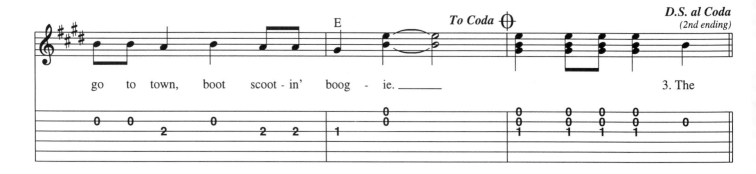

go to town, boot scoot-in' boog - ie. _____ 3. The

Coda

Chorus

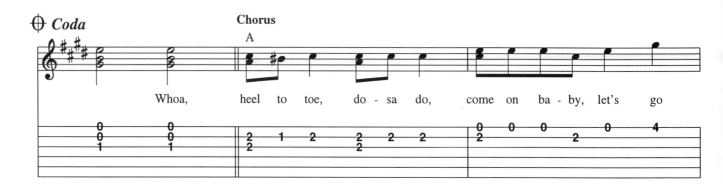

Whoa, heel to toe, do - sa do, come on ba - by, let's go

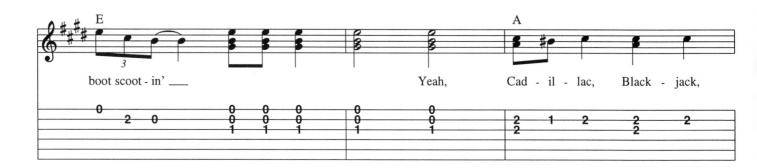

boot scoot - in' ___ Yeah, Cad - il - lac, Black - jack,

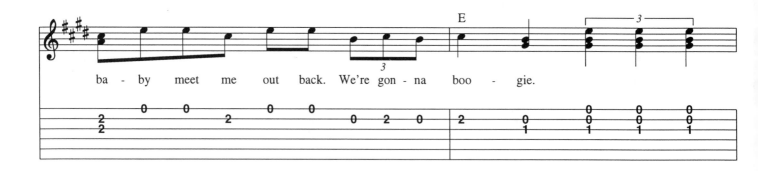

ba - by meet me out back. We're gon - na boo - gie.

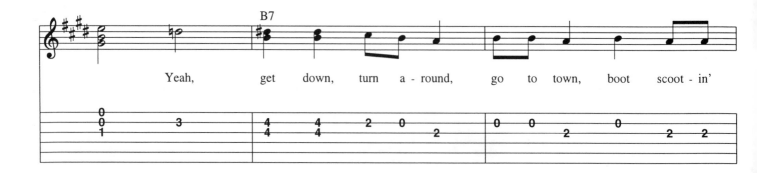

Yeah, get down, turn a - round, go to town, boot scoot - in'

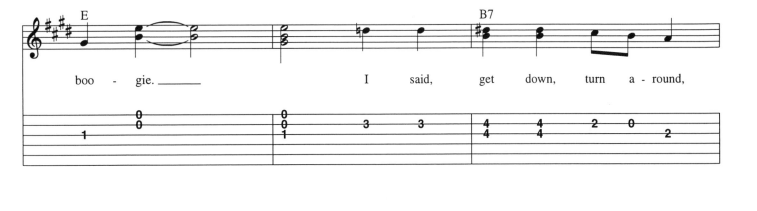

boo - gie. _____ I said, get down, turn a - round,

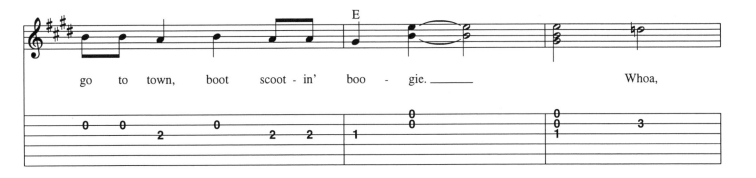

go to town, boot scoot - in' boo - gie. _____ Whoa,

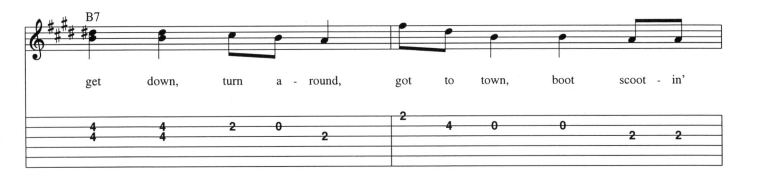

get down, turn a - round, got to town, boot scoot - in'

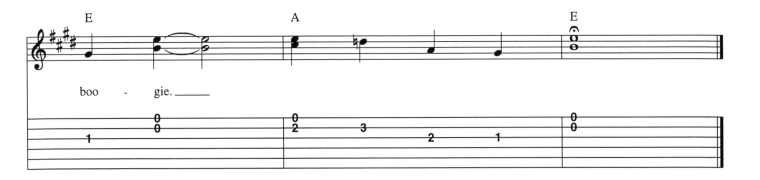

boo - gie. _____

Chattahoochee

Words and Music by Jim McBride and Alan Jackson

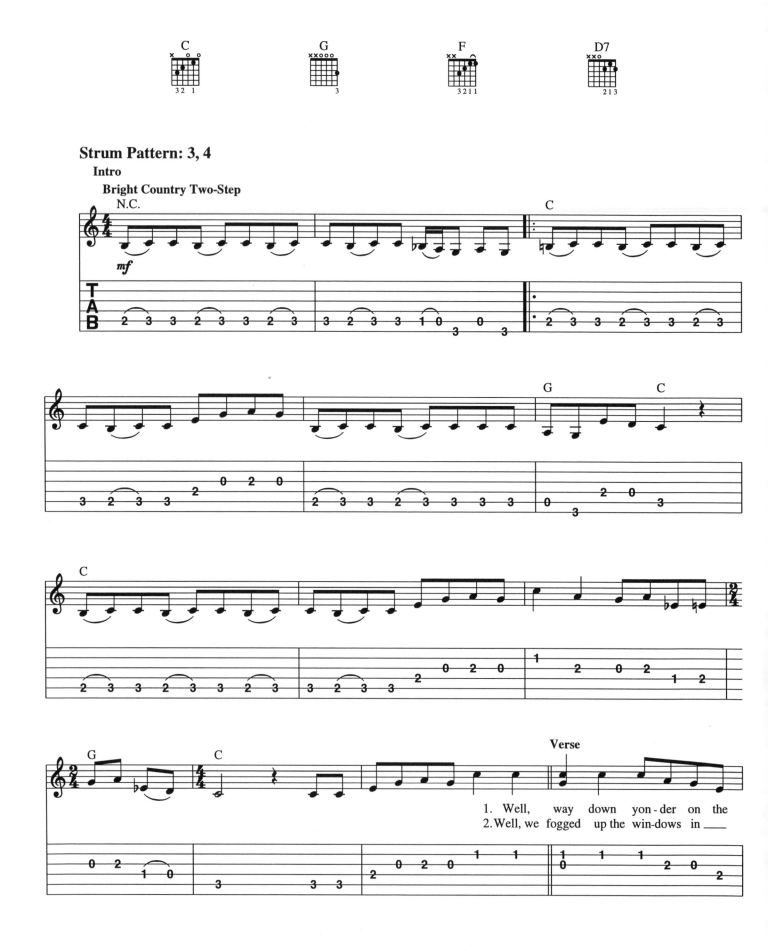

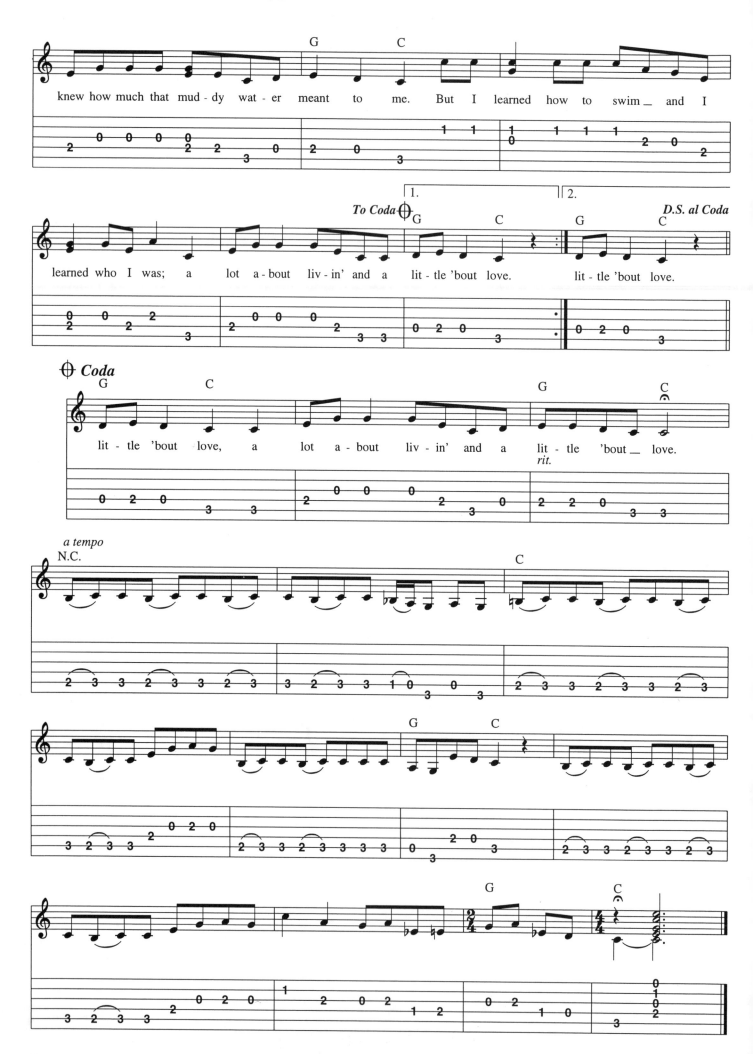

Don't Speak

Words and Music by Eric Stefani and Gwen Stefani

Strum Pattern: 2
Pick Pattern: 2

Intro
Moderately

Verse

1. You and me, we used to be to-geth-er,

ev-'ry day to-geth-er, al - ways. I real-ly feel that I'm

los - ing my best friend. I can't be - lieve this could be the end. It

Pre-Chorus

looks as though you're let-ting go, and if it's real, well, I don't want to know.

See Additional Lyrics

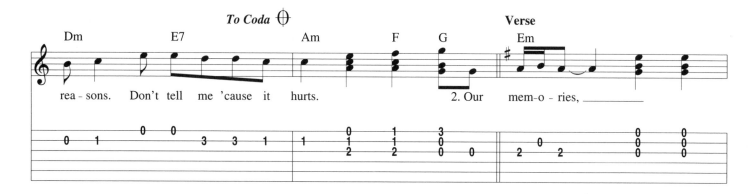

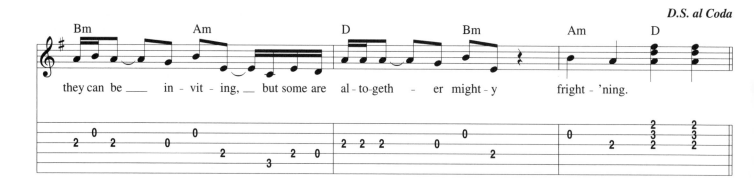

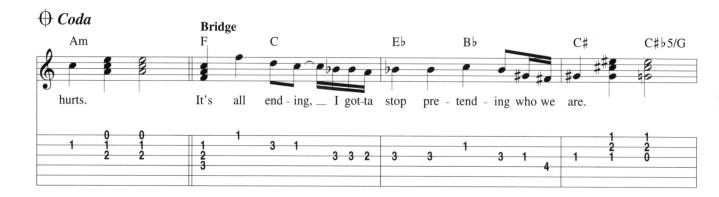

Additional Lyrics

Pre-Chorus As we die, both you and I,
With my head in my hands I sit and cry.

Counting Blue Cars

Words by J.R. Richards
Music by Scot Alexander, George Pendergast,
Rodney Browning, J. R. Richards and Gregory Kolanek

Strum Pattern: 2
Pick Pattern: 2

Verse
Moderate Rock

1. Must have been late af-ter-noon.
2., 3. *See Additional Lyrics*

I could tell by how far ___ the child's shad-ow stretched out. And he ___ walked with a pur-pose in his sneak-ers down the street. _ He had

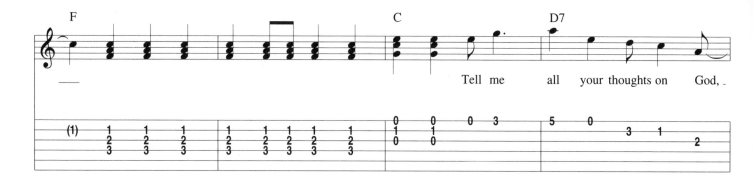

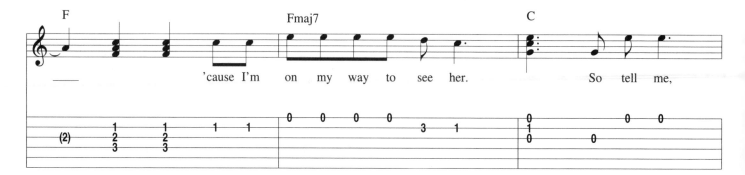

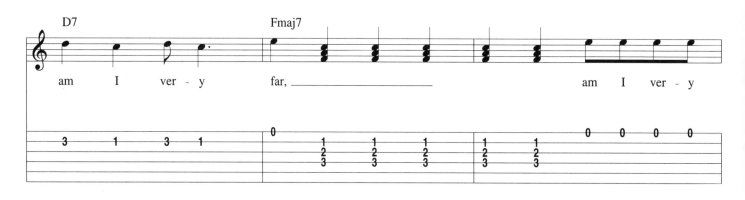

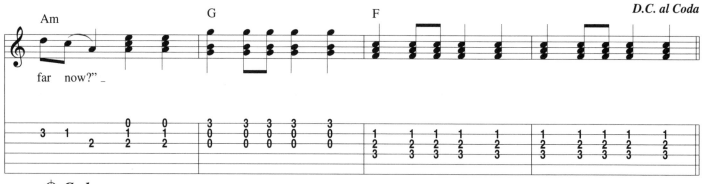

Additional Lyrics

2. Must have been late afternoon.
   On our way, the sun broke free of the clouds.
   We count only blue cars, skip the cracks in the street
   And ask many questions like children often do.

3. It's getting cold, picked up the pace.
   How our shoes make hard noises in this place.
   Our clothes are stained, we pass money, cross our people
   And ask many questions like children often do.

Danny Boy (Londonderry Air)

Words by Frederick Edward Weatherly
Traditional Irish Folk Melody

Strum Pattern: 4
Pick Pattern: 4

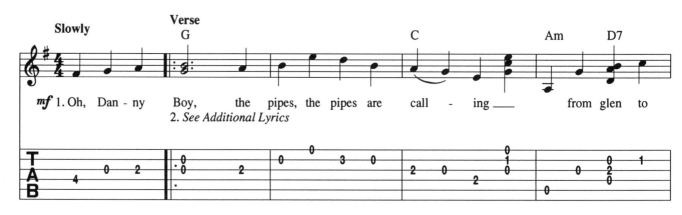

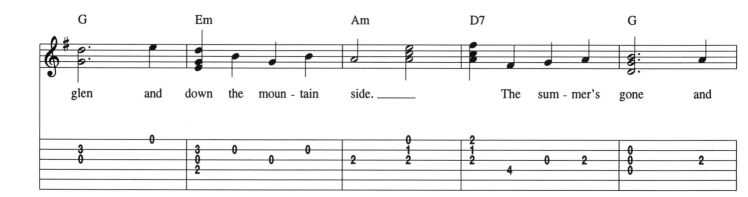

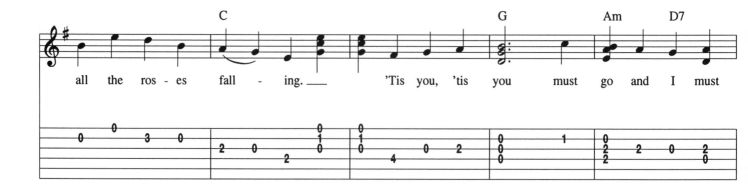

Additional Lyrics

2. And when ye come and all the flowers are dying,
   If I am dead, and dead I well may be,
   You'll come and find the place where I am lying,
   And kneel and say an Ave there for me.

Chorus And I shall hear, tho' soft you tread above me.
   And all my grave will warmer, sweeter be.
   If you will bend and tell me that you love me
   Then I shall sleep in peace until you come to me.

Don't Get Around Much Anymore

Words and Music by Bob Russell and Duke Ellington

El Shaddai

Words and Music by Michael Card and John Thompson

Strum Pattern: 2, 3
Pick Pattern: 2, 4

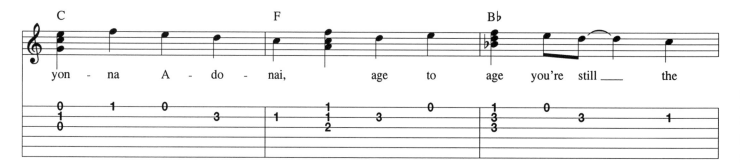

El - Shad - dai, _____ El - Shad - dai, _____ El - El -

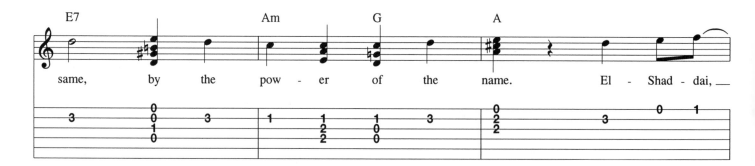

yon - na A - do - nai, age to age you're still ___ the

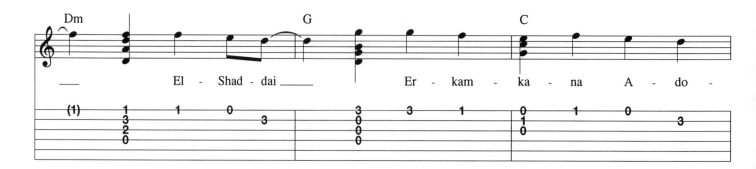

same, by the pow - er of the name. El - Shad - dai, _

_ El - Shad - dai _____ Er - kam - ka - na A - do -

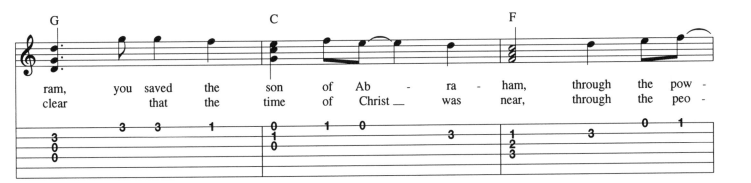

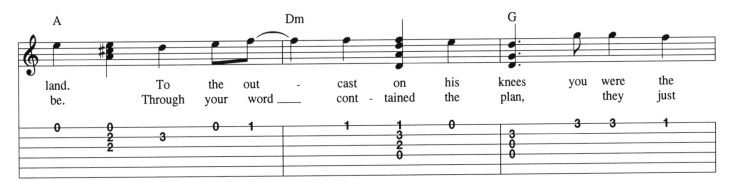

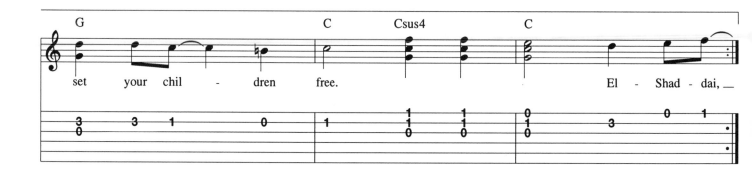

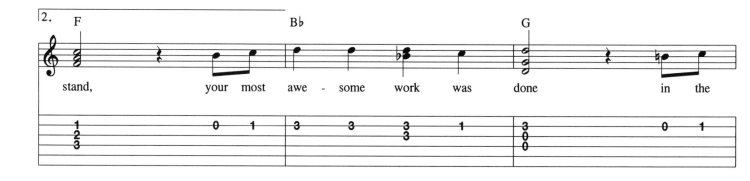

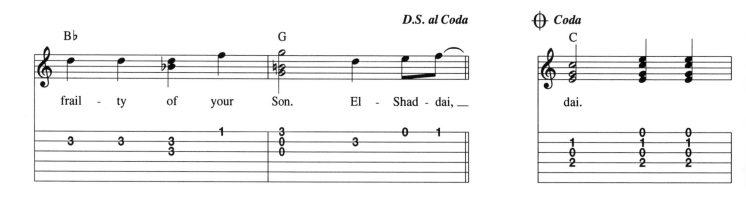

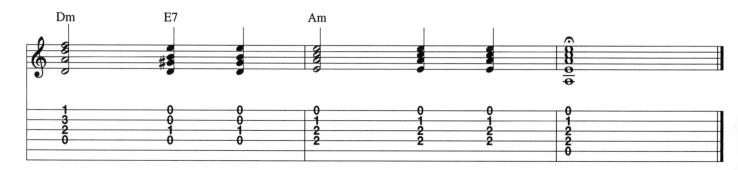

Great Balls of Fire

Words and Music by Otis Blackwell and Jack Hammer

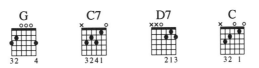

Strum Pattern: 1, 2
Pick Pattern: 2, 4

Intro

Bright Rock

You came a-long and you moved __ me, hon-ey.   I changed my mind,

love's just fine. __   Good-ness gra-cious, great __ balls of fire!

Instrumental ends

Bridge

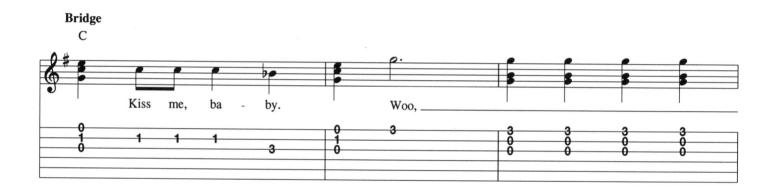

Kiss me, ba - by.   Woo, _____

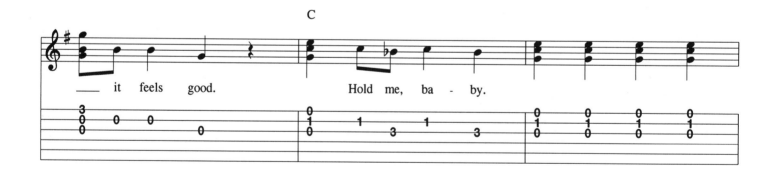

___ it feels good.   Hold me, ba - by.

Girl, just let me love you like a lov - er should. __
I want to love you like a lov - er should. __   You're fine, ____

so kind, ___ I'm gon-na tell the world that you're mine, mine, mine, mine. ___

Outro

I chew my nails and I twid-dle my thumb. ___ I'm real ner-vous but it

sure is fun. ___ Come on, ba - by, you're driv - ing me cra - zy.

1.

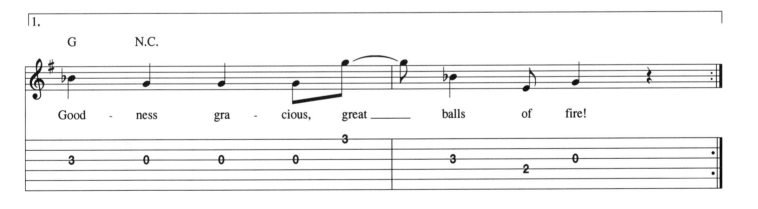

Good - ness gra - cious, great ___ balls of fire!

2.

Good - ness gra - cious, great ___ balls of fire!

Free Bird

Words and Music by Allen Collins and Ronnie Van Zant

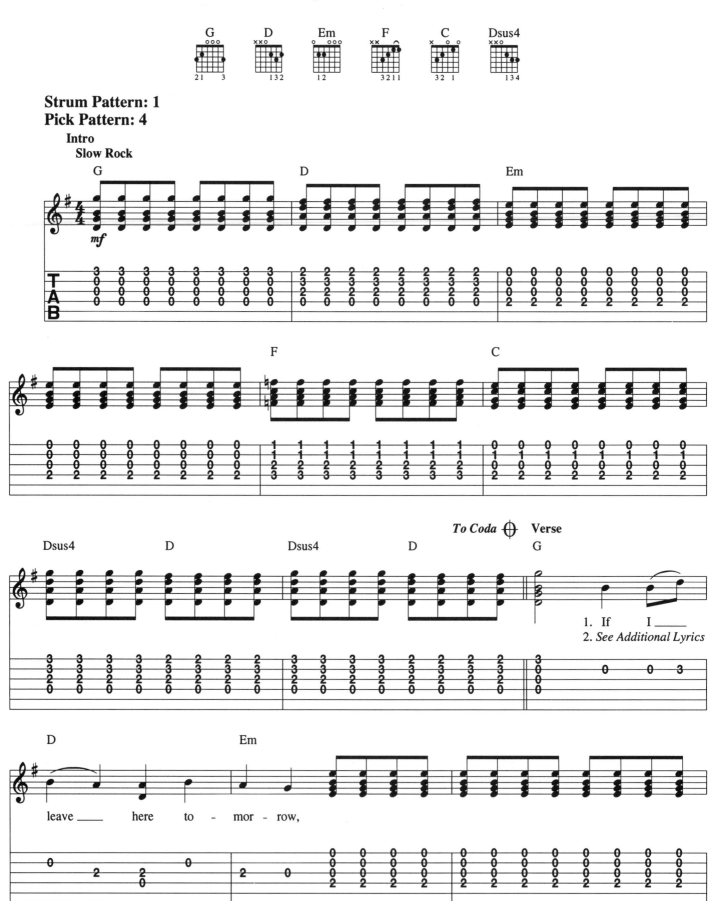

Strum Pattern: 1
Pick Pattern: 4

© Copyright 1973, 1975 by MCA - DUCHESS MUSIC CORPORATION and
WINDSWEPT PACIFIC ENTERTAINMENT CO. d/b/a LONGITUDE MUSIC CO.
International Copyright Secured   All Rights Reserved
MCA Music Publishing

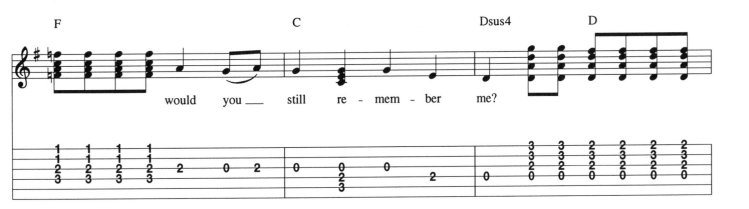

would you ___ still re - mem - ber me?

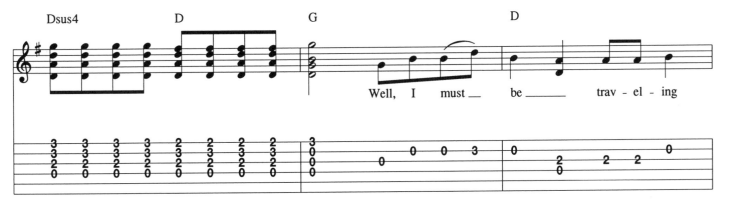

Well, I must ___ be _____ trav - el - ing

on now, 'cause there's too man - y plac - es I've got to

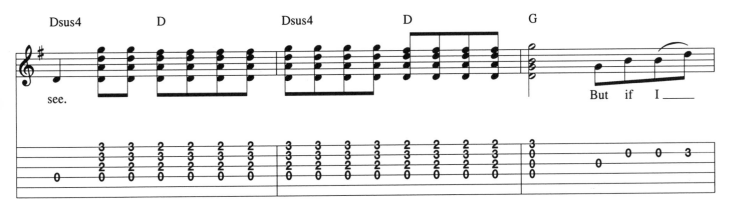

see. But if I ____

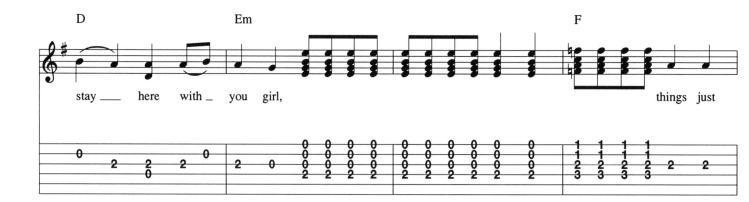

stay ___ here with _ you girl,   things just

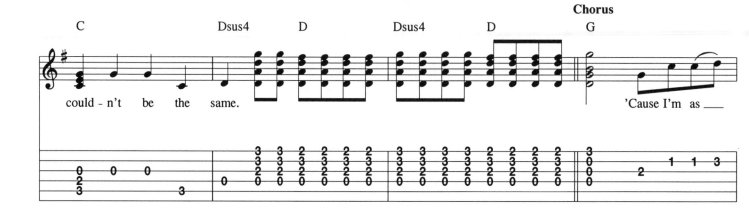

could - n't be the same.   **Chorus**   'Cause I'm as ___

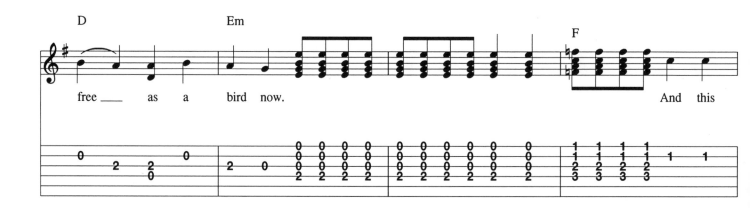

free ___ as a bird now.   And this

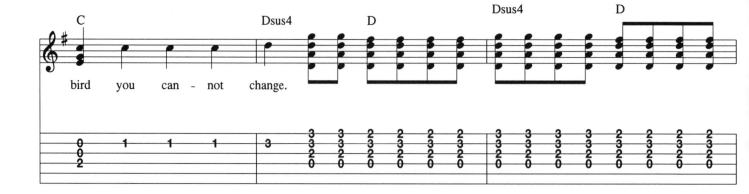

bird you can - not change.

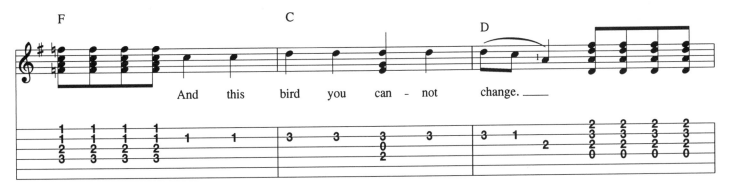

And this bird you can - not change. _____

And this bird you can - not change.

Lord _ knows, I can't _ change.

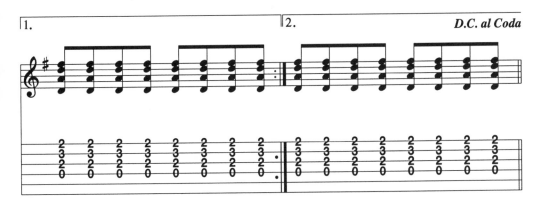

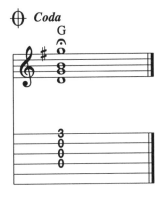

Additonal Lyrics

2. Bye, bye baby, it's been sweet now, yeah, yeah,
   Though this feelin' I can't change.
   A please don't take it so badly,
   'Cause the Lord knows I'm to blame.
   But if I stay here with you girl,
   Things just couldn't be the same.

Greensleeves

Sixteenth Century Traditional English

Strum Pattern: 7
Pick Pattern: 7

Mission: Impossible Theme

From The Paramount Motion Picture MISSION: IMPOSSIBLE

By Lalo Schifrin

The Munster's Theme

By Jack Marshall

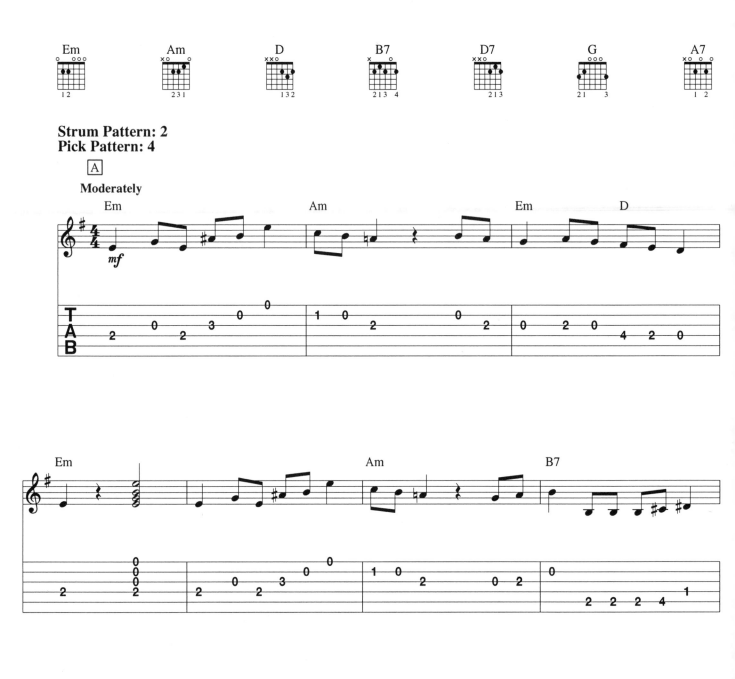

Strum Pattern: 2
Pick Pattern: 4

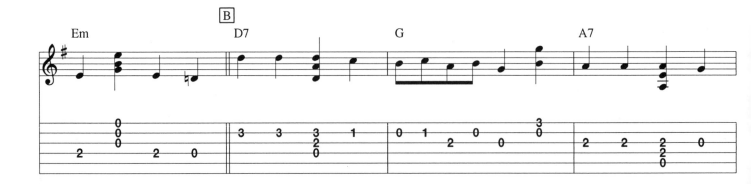

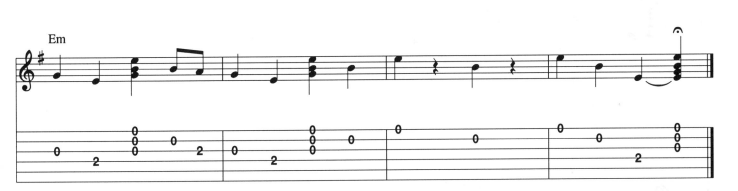

My One and Only Love

Words by Robert Mellin
Music by Guy Wood

Strum Pattern: 4
Pick Pattern: 5

Verse
Slowly

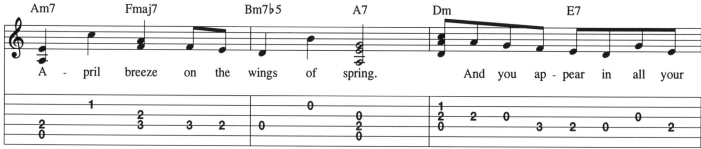

1. The ver-y thought of you makes my heart sing like an
2., 3. *See Additional Lyrics*

A-pril breeze on the wings of spring. And you ap-pear in all your

splen-dor, _____ my one and on-ly love. _____

my one and on-ly love. _____ The

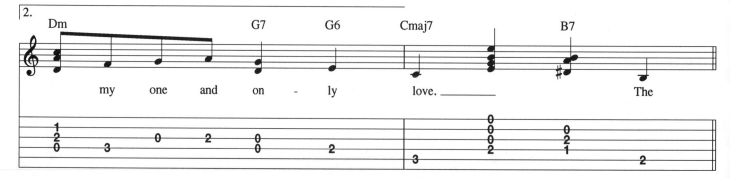

Bridge

touch of your hand is like heav - en, _____ a heav - en that I've nev - er

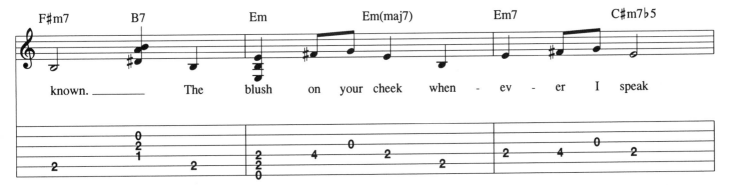

known. _____ The blush on your cheek when - ev - er I speak

D.C. al Coda

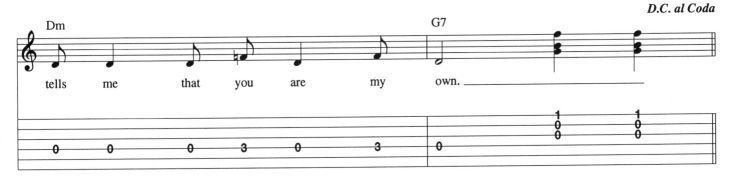

tells me that you are my own. _____

⊕ *Coda*

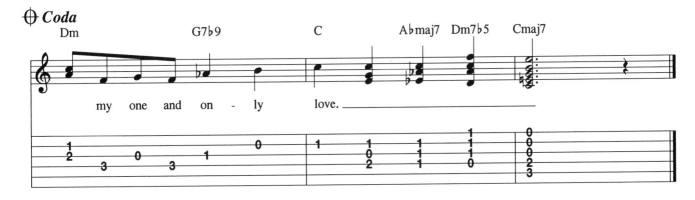

my one and on - ly love. _____

Additional Lyrics

2. The shadows fall and spread their mystic charms
   In the hush of the night while you're in my arms.
   I feel your lips so warm and tender,
   My one and only love.

3. You fill my eager heart with such desire.
   Ev'ry kiss you give sets my soul on fire.
   I give myself in sweet surrender,
   My one and only love.

Only Wanna Be with You

Words and Music by Darius Carlos Rucker, Everett Dean Felber, Mark William Bryan, and James George Sonefeld

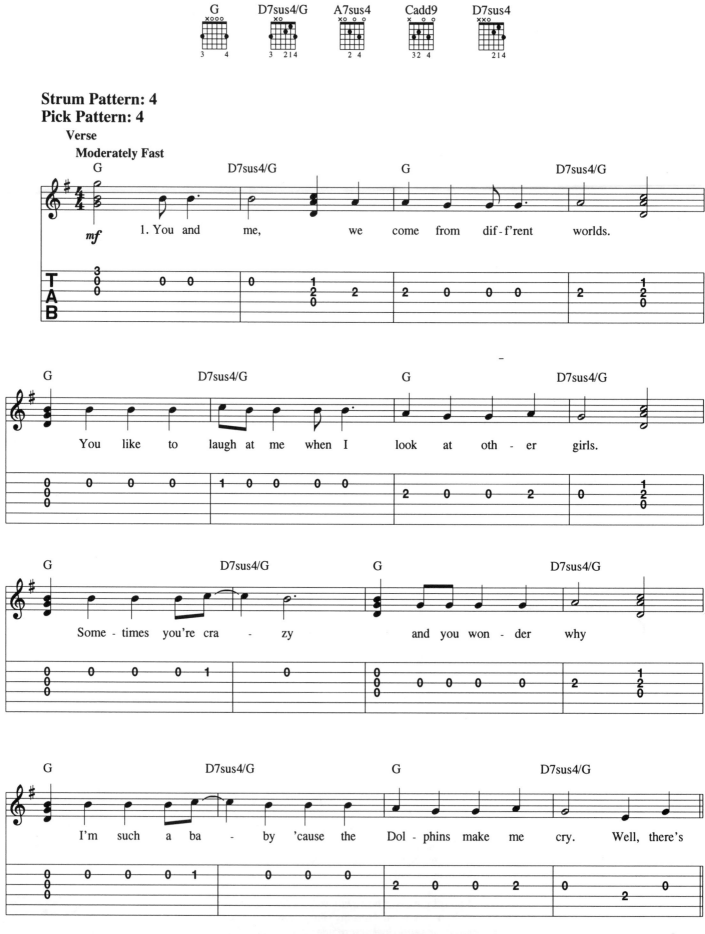

Strum Pattern: 4
Pick Pattern: 4

Chorus

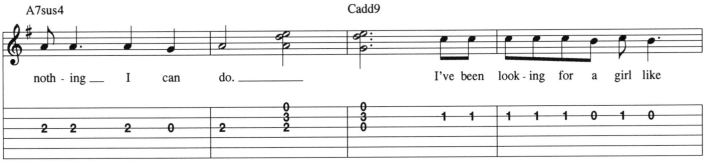

Verse

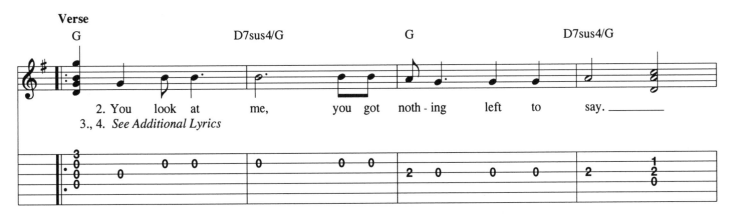

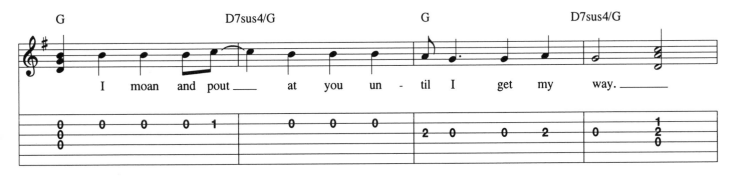

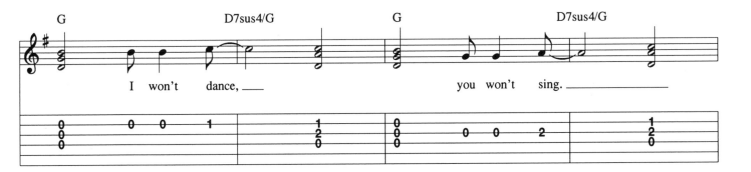

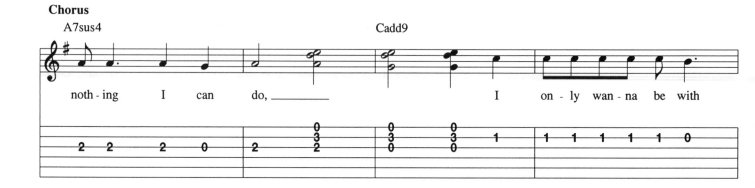

Chorus

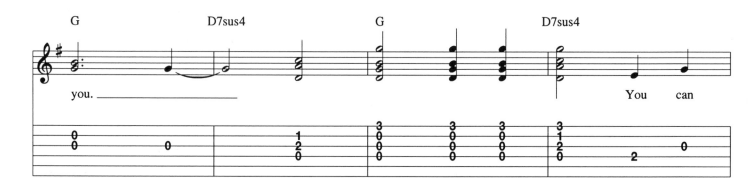

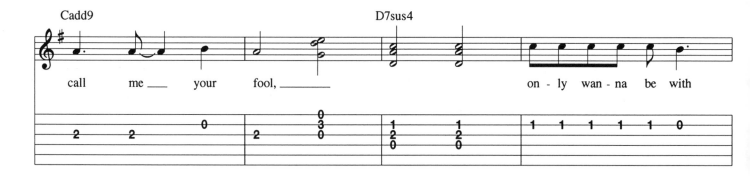

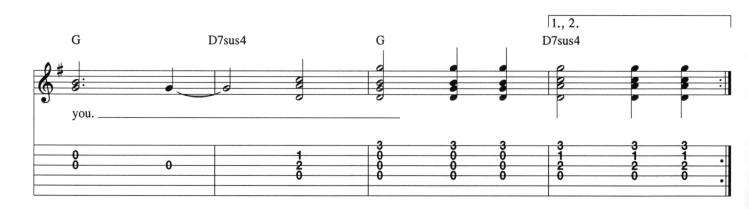

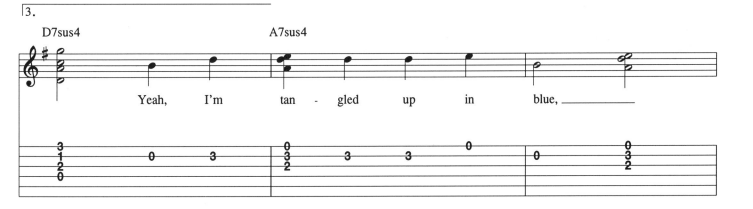

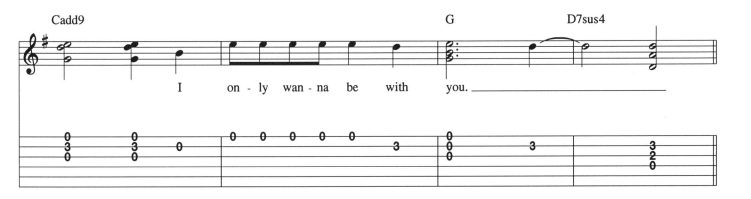

Repeat and Fade

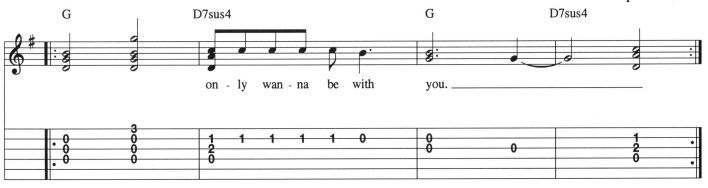

Additional Lyrics

3. Put on a little Dylan, sitting on a fence.
   I say, "That line is great." You ask me what I meant by,
   "Said I shot a man named Gray, took his wife to Italy.
   She inherit a million bucks and when she died it came to me,
   I can't help it if I'm lucky." Only wanna be with you.
   Ain't Bobby so cool? Only wanna be with you.

4. Sometimes I wonder if it will ever end.
   You get so mad at me when I go out with my friends.
   Sometimes you're crazy and you wonder why
   I'm such a baby, yeah, the Dolphins make me cry.
   Well, there's nothing I can do, only wanna be with you.
   You can call me your fool, only wanna be with you.

Rock Around the Clock

By Max C. Freedman and Jimmy DeKnight

have some fun when the clock strikes one. __ We're gon - na rock a - round the

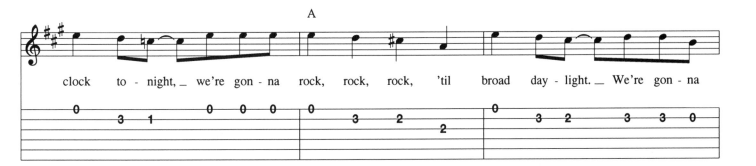

clock to - night, __ we're gon - na rock, rock, rock, 'til broad day - light. __ We're gon - na

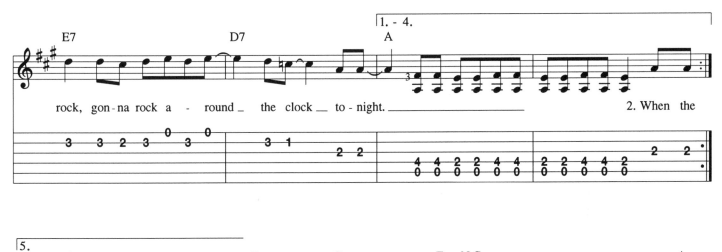

rock, gon - na rock a - round __ the clock __ to - night. _____ 2. When the

Additional Lyrics

2. When the clock strikes two, and three and four,
   If the band slows down we'll yell for more.
   We're gonna rock around the clock tonight,
   We're gonna rock, rock, rock, 'til broad daylight.
   We're gonna rock, gonna rock around the clock tonight.

3. When the chimes ring five and six and seven,
   We'll be rockin' up in seventh heav'n.
   We're gonna rock around the clock tonight,
   We're gonna rock, rock, rock, 'til broad daylight.
   We're gonna rock, gonna rock around the clock tonight.

4. When it's eight, nine, ten, eleven, too,
   I'll be goin' strong and so will you.
   We're gonna rock around the clock tonight,
   We're gonna rock, rock, rock, 'til broad daylight.
   We're gonna rock, gonna rock around the clock tonight.

5. When the clock strikes twelve, we'll cool off, then,
   Start a rockin' 'round the clock again.
   We're gonna rock around the clock tonight,
   We're gonna rock, rock, rock, 'til broad daylight.
   We're gonna rock, gonna rock around the clock tonight.

Sweet Home Chicago

Words and Music by Robert Johnson

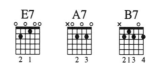

Strum Pattern: 3
Pick Pattern: 3

Intro

Verse

1. Oh, _____ ba - by, don't you want to go? ____
5. See Additional Lyrics

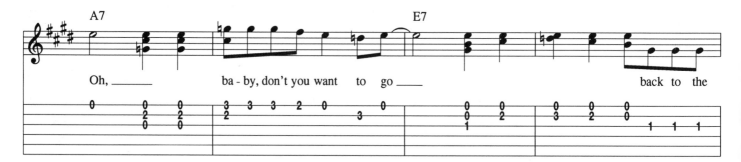

Oh, _____ ba - by, don't you want to go ____ back to the

To Coda

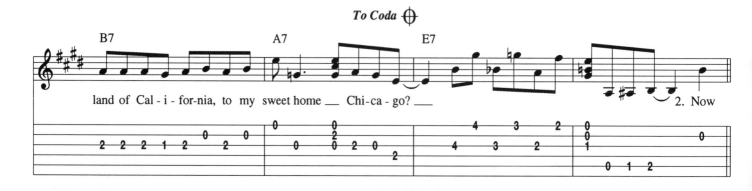

land of Cal - i - for - nia, to my sweet home ___ Chi - ca - go? ____   2. Now

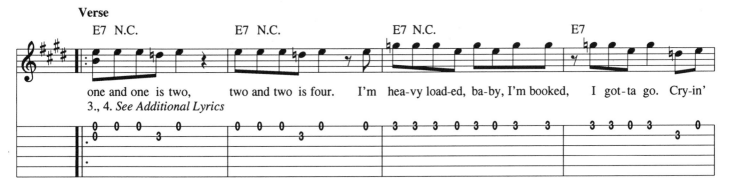

one and one is two, two and two is four. I'm hea-vy load-ed, ba-by, I'm booked, I got-ta go. Cry-in'
3., 4. See Additional Lyrics

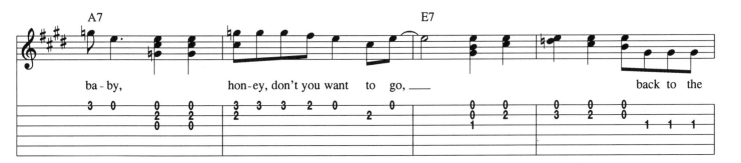

ba-by, hon-ey, don't you want to go, ___ back to the

land of Cal-i-for-nia, to my sweet home ___ Chi-ca-go? ___ 3. Now

⊕ *Coda*

Additional Lyrics

3. Now, two and two is four, four and two is six.
   You gon' keep on monkeyin' 'round here,
   Friend-boy, you gon' get your business all in a trick.
   I'm cryin' baby, honey, don't you want to go,
   Back to the land of California, to my sweet home Chicago?

4. Now, six and two is eight, eight and two is ten.
   Friend-boy, she trick you one time, sure she gon' do it again.
   I'm cryin' hey, hey, baby, don't you want to go,
   To the land of California, to my sweet home Chicago?

5. I'm goin' to California, from there to Des Moines, Iowa.
   Somebody will tell me that you need my help someday.
   Cryin' hey, hey, baby, don't you want to go,
   Back to the land of California, to my sweet home Chicago?

Vision of Love

Words and Music by Mariah Carey and Ben Margulies

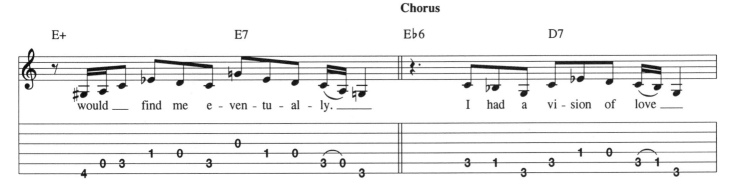

Chorus

would ___ find me e - ven - tu - al - ly. _____ I had a vi - sion of love ___

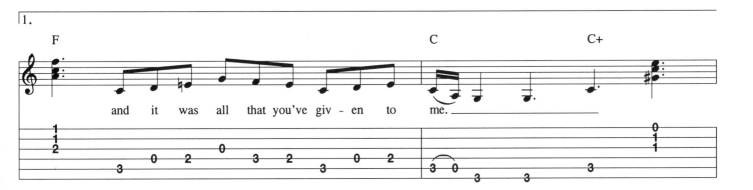

1.

and it was all that you've giv - en to me. _____

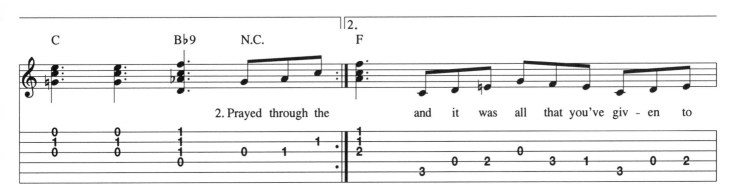

2.

2. Prayed through the and it was all that you've giv - en to

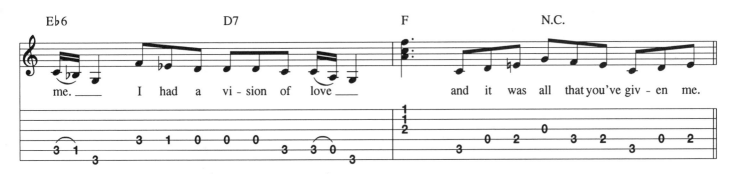

me. ____ I had a vi - sion of love ___ and it was all that you've giv - en me.

Bridge

I've re - al - ized ____ a dream, ____ mm, ____ and I vi - su - al - ized ____ the

love that came_ to be. ____ Feel __ so a - live. __ I'm so thank - ful that I've re - ceived ____ the

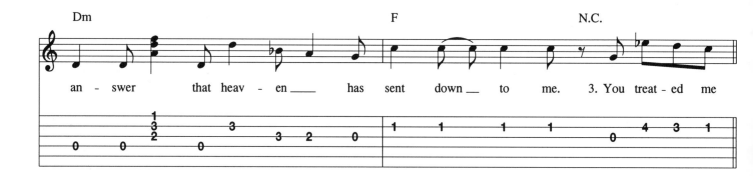

an - swer that heav - en ____ has sent down __ to me. 3. You treat - ed me

Verse

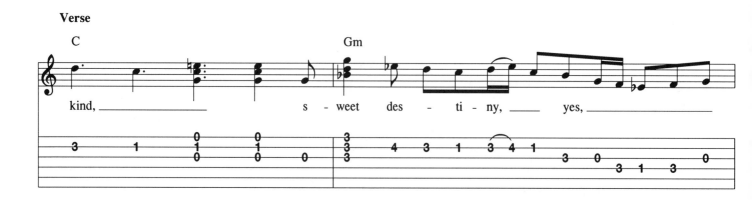

kind, _____ s - weet des - ti - ny, ____ yes, _____

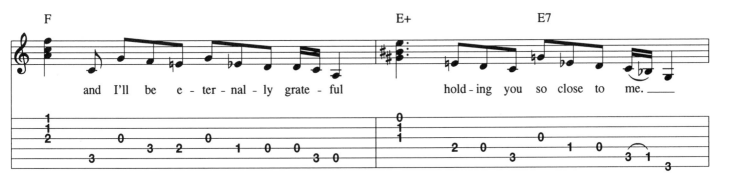

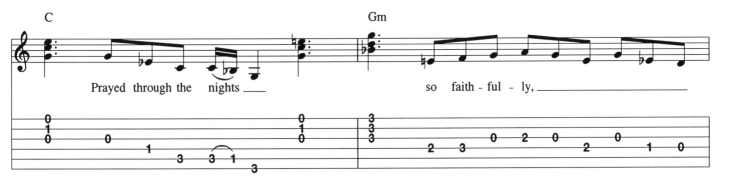

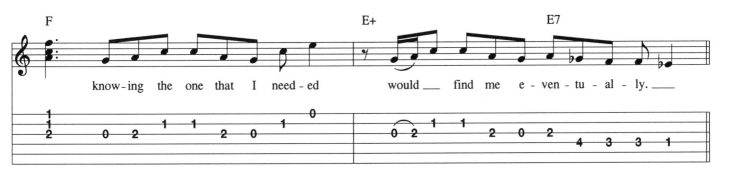

Chorus

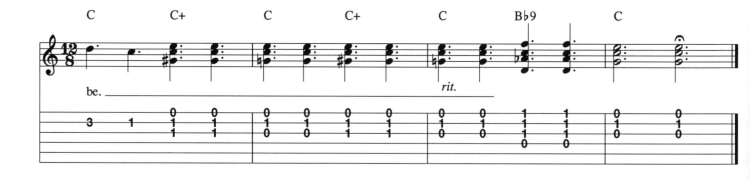

Additional Lyrics

2. Prayed through the nights.
   Felt so alone, suffered from alienation,
   Carried the weight on my own.
   Had to be strong so I believed,
   And now I know I've succeeded
   In finding the place I conceived.

Wonderwall

Words and Music by Noel Gallagher

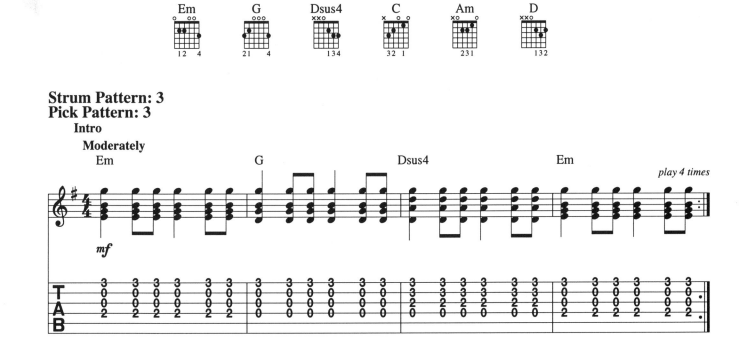

Strum Pattern: 3
Pick Pattern: 3

Intro
Moderately

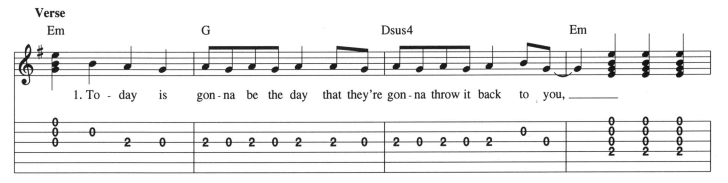

Verse

1. To-day is gon-na be the day that they're gon-na throw it back to you, ____

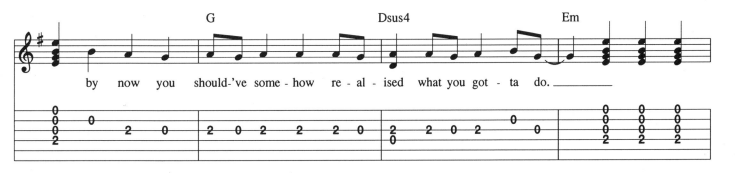

by now you should-'ve some-how re-al-ised what you got-ta do. ____

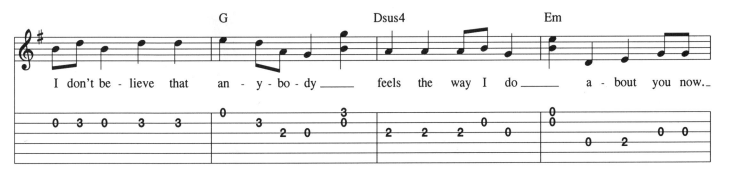

I don't be-lieve that an-y-bo-dy ____ feels the way I do ____ a-bout you now.

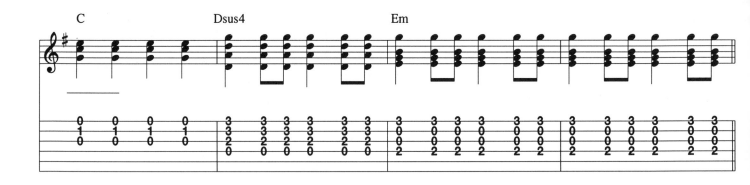

Verse

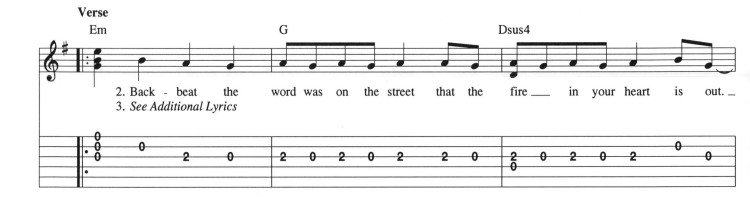

2. Back - beat the word was on the street that the fire ___ in your heart is out.
3. *See Additional Lyrics*

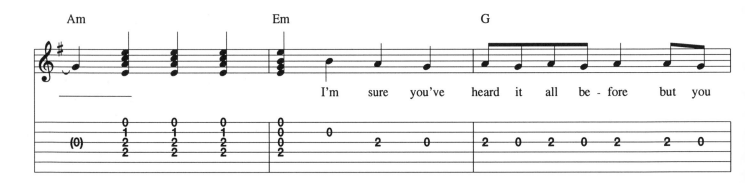

I'm sure you've heard it all be - fore but you

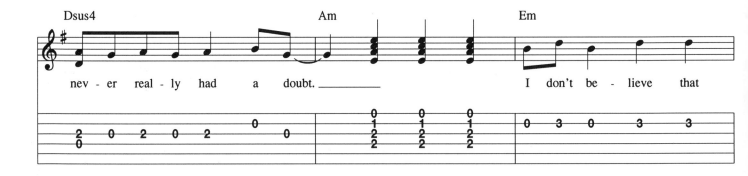

nev - er real - ly had a doubt. ___ I don't be - lieve that

an - y - bo - dy ___ feels the way I do ___ a - bout you now. ___

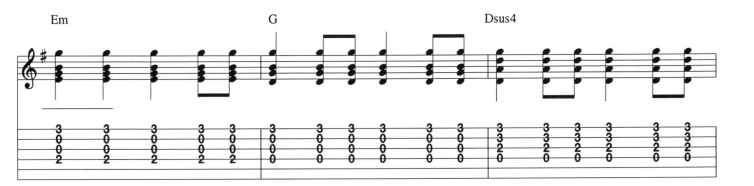

Em   G   Dsus4

Pre-Chorus

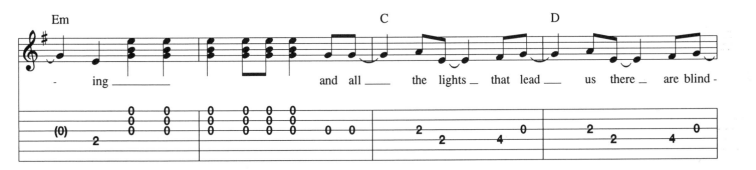

Am   C   D

And all _____ the roads _____ we have _____ to walk _____ are wind -

See Additional Lyrics

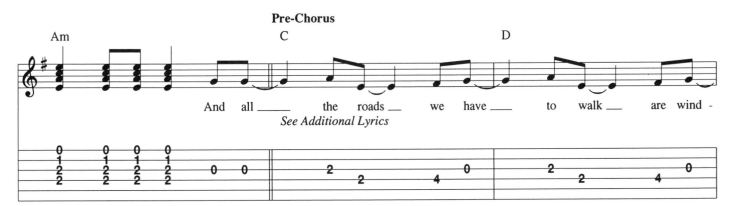

Em   C   D

- ing _____ and all _____ the lights _ that lead _ us there _ are blind -

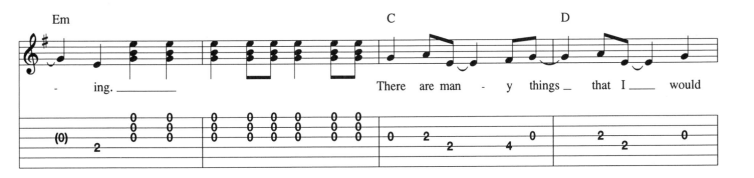

Em   C   D

- ing. _____ There are man - y things _ that I _____ would

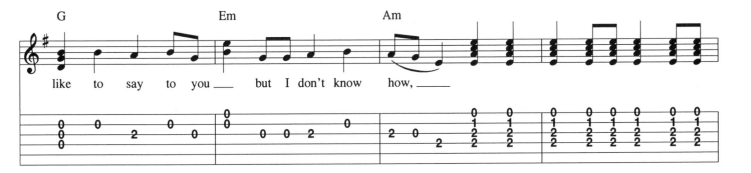

G   Em   Am

like to say to you _____ but I don't know how, _____

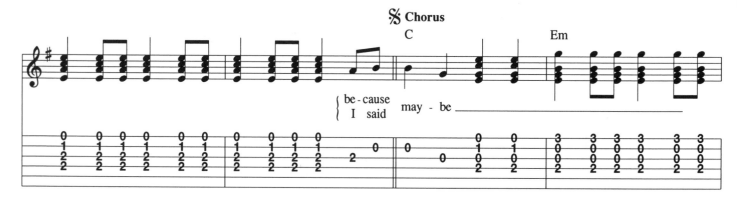

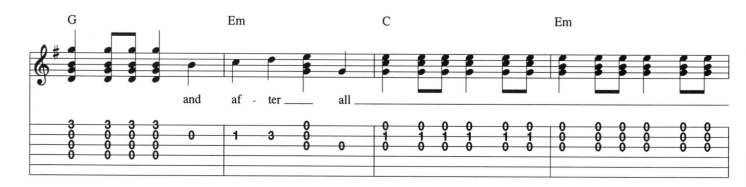

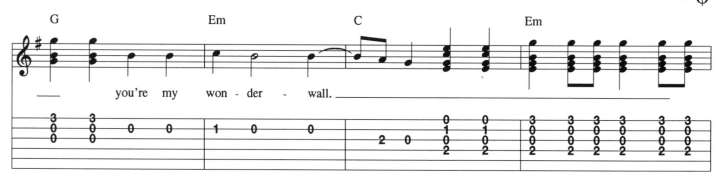

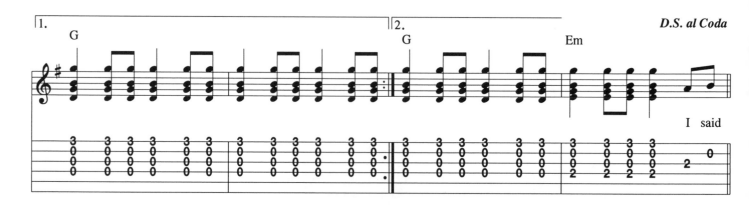

⊕ *Coda*

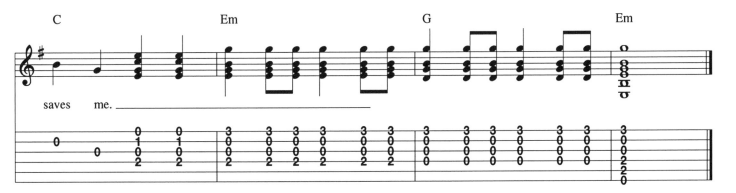

Additional Lyrics

3. Today was gonna be the day
   But they'll never throw it back to you.
   By now you should've somehow
   Realised what you're not to do.
   I don't believe that anybody
   Feels the way I do
   About you now.

Pre-Chorus And all the roads that lead you there were winding
And all the lights that light the way are blinding.
There are many things that I would like to say to you
But I don't know how.

Yesterday

Words and Music by John Lennon and Paul McCartney

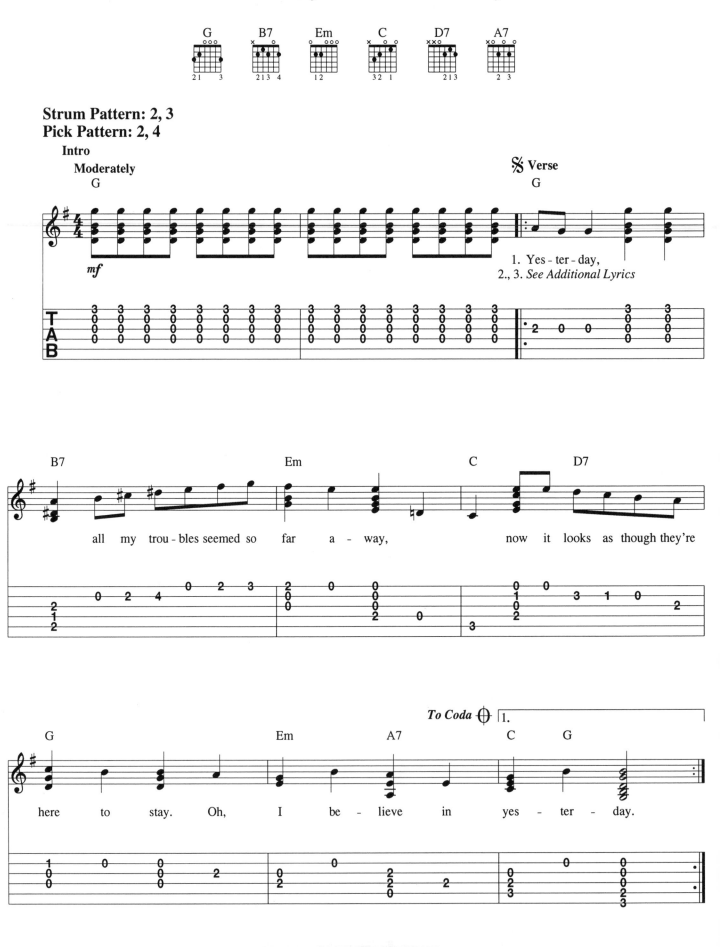

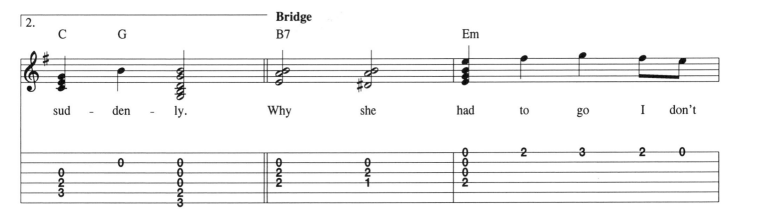

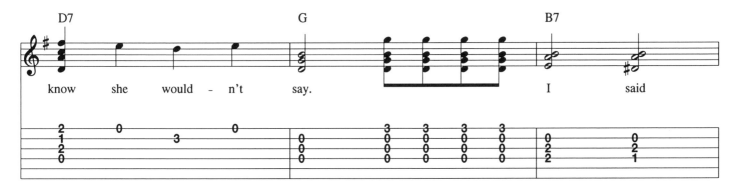

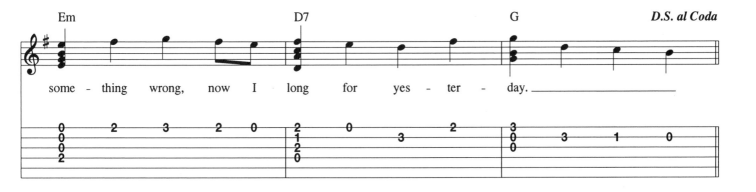

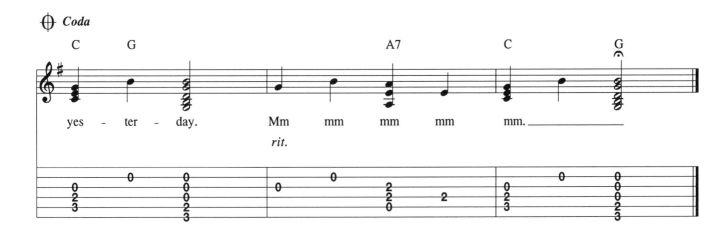

Additional Lyrics

2. Suddenly, I'm not half the man I used to be.
   There's a shadow hanging over me. Oh, yesterday came suddenly.

3. Yesterday, love was such an easy game to play.
   Now, I need a place to hide away. Oh, I believe in yesterday.

You Were Meant for Me

Words and Music by Jewel Kilcher and Steve Poltz

Strum Pattern: 2, 3
Pick Pattern: 1

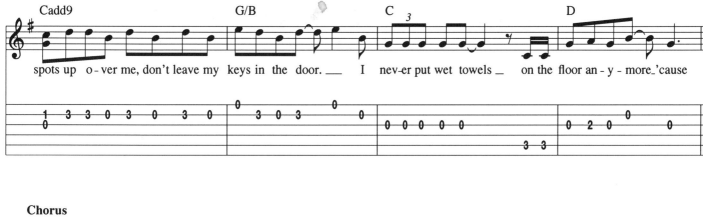

spots up o-ver me, don't leave my keys in the door. ___ I nev-er put wet towels ___ on the floor an-y-more 'cause

Chorus

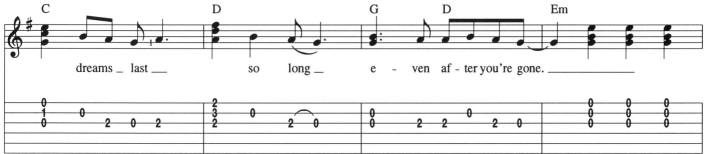

dreams ___ last ___ so long ___ e - ven af - ter you're gone. _____

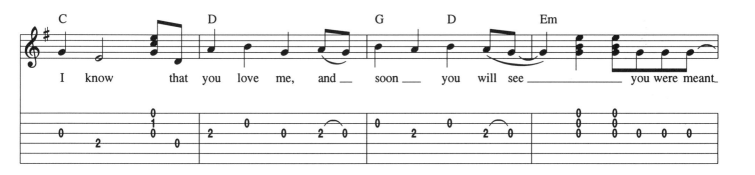

I know that you love me, and ___ soon ___ you will see _____ you were meant ___

To Coda ⊕ |1.

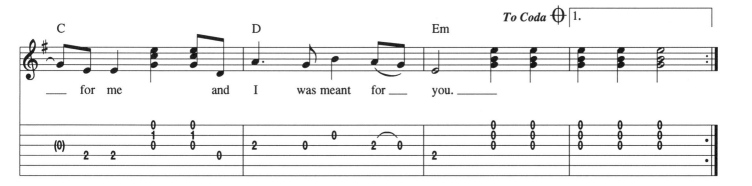

___ for me and I was meant for ___ you. _____

2.   **Bridge**

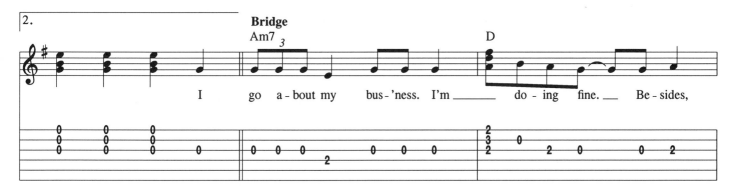

I go a-bout my bus-'ness. I'm _____ do-ing fine. ___ Be - sides,

what would I say ___ if I had you on the line. Some old sto - ry, not

D.C. al Coda
(take repeat)

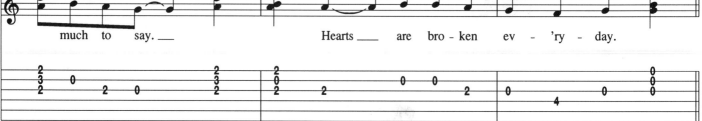

Freely

much to say. ___ Hearts ___ are bro - ken ev - 'ry - day.

⊕ Coda

Yeah, you were meant for me, and I was meant for

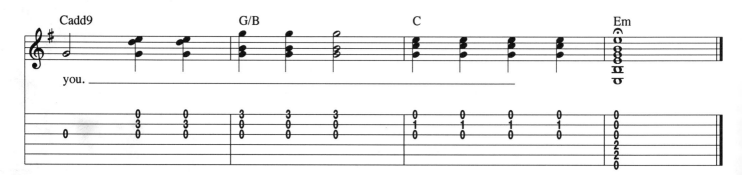

you. ___

Additional Lyrics

2. I called my mama, she was out for a walk.
Consoled a cup of coffee, but it didn't want to talk.
So, I picked up the paper, it was more bad news.
My heart's been broken by people being used.
Put on my coat in the pouring rain.
I saw a movie, it just wasn't the same 'cause
It was happy or I was sad,
And it made me miss you, oh, so bad 'cause...

3. I brush my teeth, I put the cap back on.
I know you hate it when I leave the light on.
I pick up a cup and then I turn the sheets down,
And then I take a deep breath, a good look around.
Put on my pj's and hop into bed.
I'm half alive, but I feel mostly dead.
I try and tell myself it'll be all right.
I just shouldn't think anymore tonight 'cause...

Your Song

Words and Music by Elton John and Bernie Taupin

Additonal Lyrics

2. If I was a sculptor, but then again no,
   Or a man who makes potions in a travelin' show.
   I know it's not much, but it's the best I can do.
   My gift is my song and this one's for you.

3. I sat on the roof and kicked off the moss.
   Well a few of the verses, well they've got me quite cross.
   But the sun's been quite kind while I wrote this song.
   It's for people like you that keep it turned on.

4. So excuse me forgetting, but these days I do.
   You see I've forgotten if they're green or they're blue.
   Anyway, the thing is, what I really mean,
   Yours are the sweetest eyes I've ever seen.

Achy Breaky Heart
(Don't Tell My Heart)

Words and Music by Don Von Tress

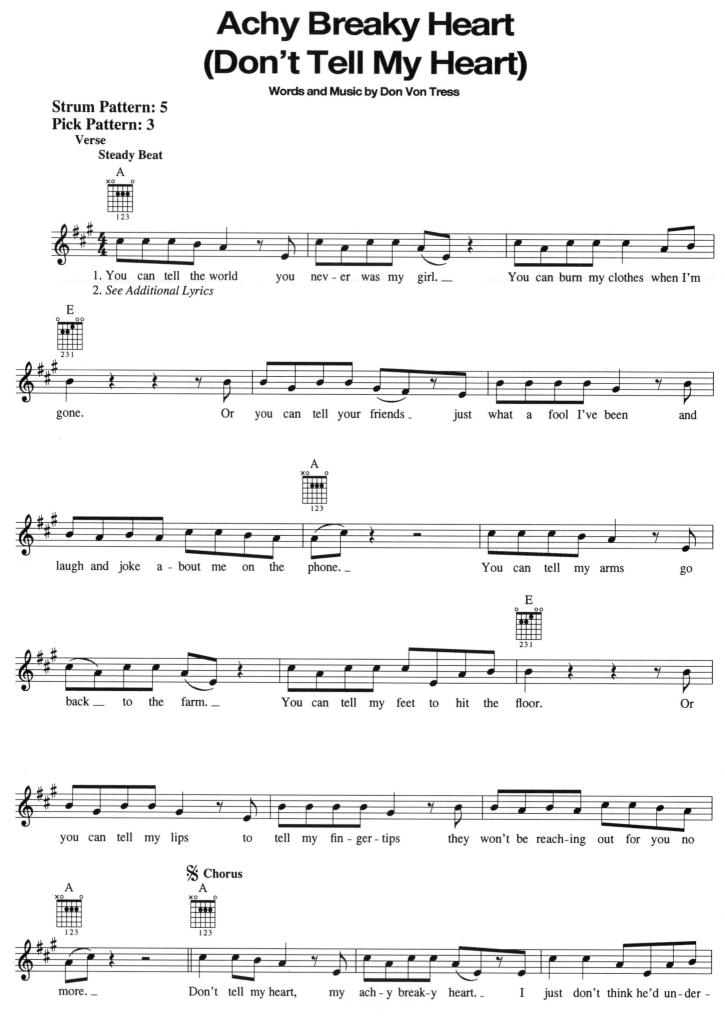

Additional Lyrics

2. You can tell your ma I moved to Arkansas.
   You can tell your dog to bite my leg.
   Or tell your brother Cliff whose fist can tell my lip,
   He never really liked me anyway.
   Or tell your Aunt Louise,
   Tell anything you please.
   Myself already knows I'm not okay.
   Or you can tell my eyes to watch out for my mind,
   It might be walking out on me today.

All My Loving

from A HARD DAY'S NIGHT

Words and Music by John Lennon and Paul McCartney

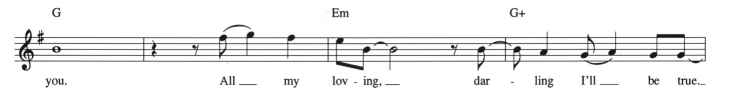

you. All ___ my lov - ing, ___ dar - ling I'll ___ be true.

To Coda ⊕

Guitar Solo

___

D.S. al Coda
(take 2nd ending)

3. Close your

⊕ *Coda*

Outro-Chorus

All ___ my lov - ing, ___ all _____ my ___

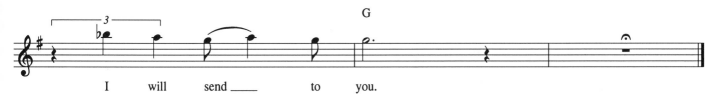

___ lov - ing, ooh, ___ all ___ my ___ lov - ing,

I will send ___ to you.

Additional Lyrics

2. I'll pretend that I'm kissing
   The lips I am missing.
   And hope that my dreams will come true.
   And then while I'm away
   I'll write home ev'ryday.
   And I'll send all my loving to you.

Are You Sleeping

Traditional

Strum Pattern: 5
Pick Pattern: 1

Moderately

| G | D7 | G | | D7 | G | | D7 | G | | D7 | G |

Are you sleep-ing, are you sleep-ing, broth-er John, broth-er John?
(French) Frè - re Jac - ques, Frè - re Jac - ques, dor - mez vous, dor - mez vous?

| D7 | G | | D7 | G | | D7 | G | | D7 | G |

Morn-ing bells are ring - ing, morn-ing bells are ring - ing, ding ding dong, ding ding dong.
Son - nez les ma - ti - nes, son - nez les ma - ti - nes, din din don, din din don.

Hello, Dolly!

Music and Lyric by Jerry Herman

Strum Pattern: 3
Pick Pattern: 3

Verse
Medium Strut

C   Am

Hel - lo, Dol - ly, well, hel - lo, Dol - ly. It's so

Cmaj7   C°7   Dm   G7

nice to have you back where you be - long. You're look - ing

Dm   Bb

swell, Dol - ly, we can tell, Dol - ly. You're still

Back In The U.S.S.R.

Words and Music by John Lennon and Paul McCartney

U. S. S. R. _____ Well, the

Bridge

U - kraine girls real - ly knock me out, they leave the _____

West be - hind. _____ And Mos - cow girls make me

sing and shout, _____ and Geor - gia's al - ways on my mi - mi - mi - mi - mi - mi -

D.C. al Coda

mi - mi - mind. _____

✛ *Coda*

Back in the U. S. S. R. _____

Additional Lyrics

2. Been away so long I hardly knew the place,
   Gee, it's good to get back home.
   Leave it 'til tomorrow to unpack my case,
   Honey disconnect the phone.

3. Show me 'round your snow peacked mountains way down south,
   Take me to your daddy's farm.
   Let me hear your balalaikas ringing out,
   Come and keep your comrade warm.

Ave Maria

By Franz Schubert

Strum Pattern: 1
Pick Pattern: 2

Verse
Reverently

Beauty and the Beast

from Walt Disney's BEAUTY AND THE BEAST
Lyrics by Howard Ashman
Music by Alan Menken

Born To Be Wild

Words and Music by Mars Bonfire

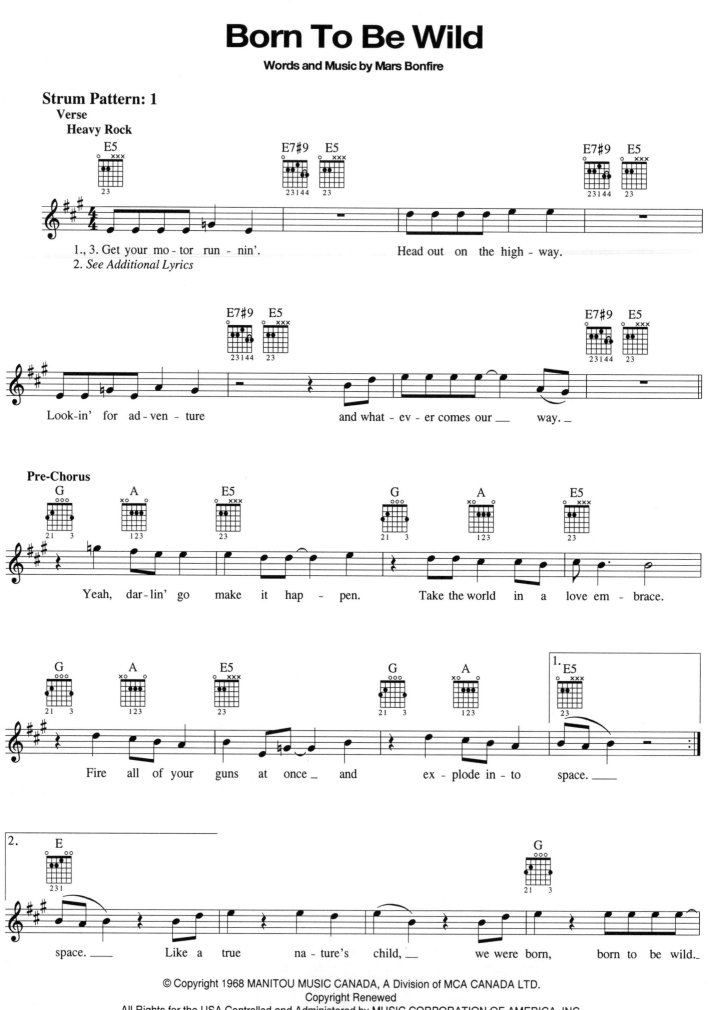

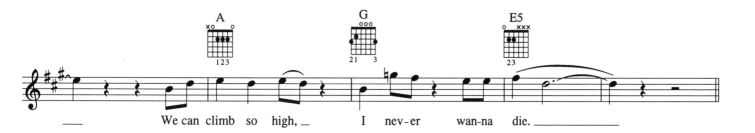

We can climb so high, _ I nev-er wan-na die. _____

Chorus

Born to be wild. _____

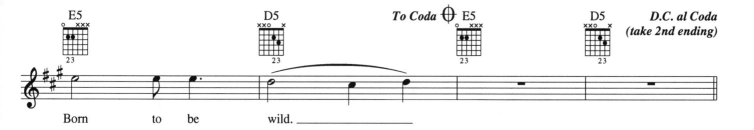

To Coda ⊕

D.C. al Coda
(take 2nd ending)

Born to be wild. _____

⊕ *Coda*

Outro

Repeat and Fade

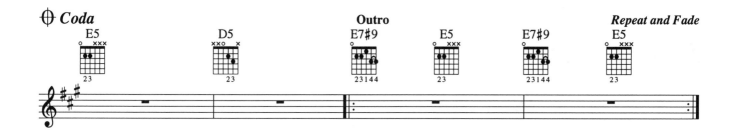

Additional Lyrics

2. I like smoke and lightning,
   Heavy metal thunder,
   Racin' with the wind,
   And the feelin' that I'm under.

The Boys Are Back In Town

Words and Music by Philip Parris Lynott

Additional Lyrics

2. You know that chick that used to dance a lot?
Every night she'd be on the floor shaking what she'd got.
Man, when I tell you she was cool, she was hot.
I mean she was steaming.
And that time over at Johnny's place.
Well, this chick got up and she slapped Johnny's face.
Man, we just fell about the place.
If that chick don't wanna know, forget her.

3. Friday night they'll be dressed to kill
Down at Dino's Bar and Grill.
The drink will flow and blood will spill.
And if the boys want to fight, you better let 'em.
That jukebox in the corner blasting out my favorite song.
The nights are getting warmer, it won't be long.
It won't be long till summer comes
Now that the boys are here again.

Crazy

Words and Music by Willie Nelson

Edelweiss

from THE SOUND OF MUSIC
Lyrics by Oscar Hammerstein II
Music by Richard Rodgers

Friends in Low Places

Words and Music by Dewayne Blackwell and Earl Bud Lee

Strum Pattern: 6
Pick Pattern: 6

Additional Lyrics

2. Well, I guess I was wrong, I just don't belong,
   But then, I've been there before.
   Ev'rything's alright, I'll just say goodnight,
   And I'll show myself to the door.
   Hey, I didn't mean to cause a big scene,
   Just give me an hour and then,
   Well, I'll be as high as that ivory tower that you're livin' in.

Have I Told You Lately

Words and Music by Van Morrison

and some-how you make it bet-ter, ease my trou-bles that's ___ what you do.

Bridge

There's a love that's di-vine and it's yours and it's mine _____ like the sun.

And at the end of the day we should give thanks and pray ___

1.
to the one, ___ to the one. ___

2.
Have I to the one. ___ And have I

D.S. al Coda

Coda

do. Take a-way all ___ my sad-ness, fill my life with glad-ness,

ease my trou-bles that's ___ what you do. Take a-way all ___ my sad-ness,

fill my heart with glad-ness, ease my trou-bles that's ___ what you do. _____

rit.

He's Got the Whole World in His Hands

African-American Folksong

Strum Pattern: 2
Pick Pattern: 4

Additional Lyrics

2. He's got the wind and the rain
In His hands,
He's got the wind and the rain
In His hands,
He's got the wind and the rain
In His hands,
He's got the whole world in His hands.

3. He's got the wee small baby
In His hands,
And He's got all you lovers
In His hands,
Oh, He's got everybody
In His hands,
He's got the whole world in His hands.

House of the Rising Sun

Traditional

Strum Pattern: 8
Pick Pattern: 8

Additional Lyrics

2. Go speak to my baby sister and say,
"Don't do as I have done."
Stay away from places like this one in New Orleans
They call the Rising Sun.

Home on the Range

Lyrics by Dr. Brewster Higley
Music by Dan Kelly

Strum Pattern: 7
Pick Pattern: 9

Layla

Words and Music by Eric Clapton and Jim Gordon

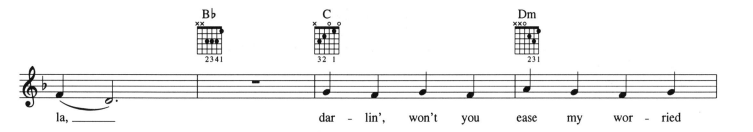

la, _____   dar - lin', won't you ease my wor - ried

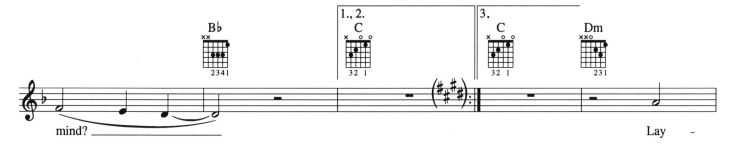

mind? _____   Lay -

Outro

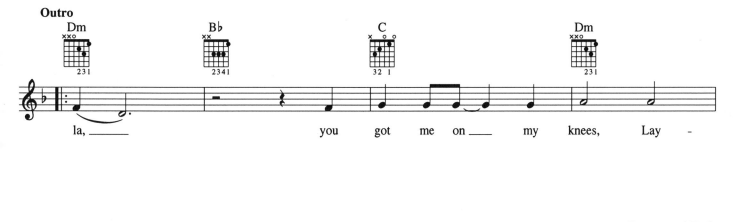

la, _____   you got me on ___ my knees, Lay -

Repeat and Fade

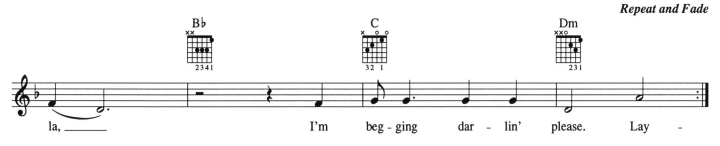

la, _____   I'm beg - ging dar - lin' please. Lay -

Additional Lyrics

2. Tried to give you consolation.
   Your old man won't let you down.
   Like a fool I fell in love with you,
   Turned the whole world upside down.

3. Let's make the best of the situation,
   Before I fin'ly go insane.
   Please don't say we'll never find a way,
   And tell me all my love's in vain.

Let It Be

Words and Music by John Lennon and Paul McCartney

be,   let it be.   Let it be, _____ let it be.

To Coda ⊕   *D.S. al Coda*

Whis - per words of wis - dom,   let it be. _____   3. And

⊕ *Coda*   **Outro**

be. _____

Additional Lyrics

2. And when the broken hearted people
   Living in the world agree,
   There will be an answer, let it be.
   For tho' they may be parted
   There is still a chance that they will see,
   There will be an answer, let it be.

3. And when the night is cloudy
   There is still a light that shines on me,
   Shine until tomorrow, let it be.
   I wake up to the sound of music
   Mother Mary comes to me,
   Speaking words of wisdom, let it be.

Love Me Do

Words and Music by John Lennon and Paul McCartney

Strum Pattern: 5
Pick Pattern: 3
    Intro
    Moderate Rock

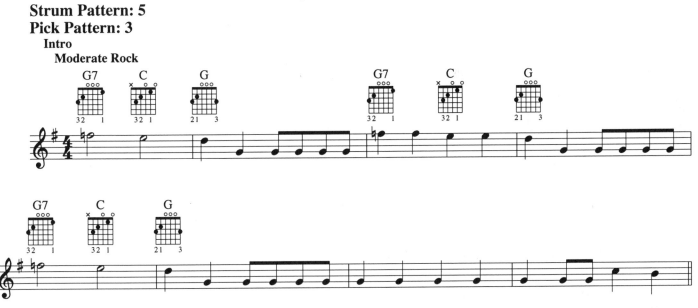

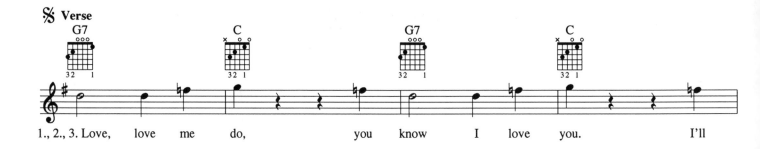

Verse

1., 2., 3. Love, love me do, you know I love you. I'll

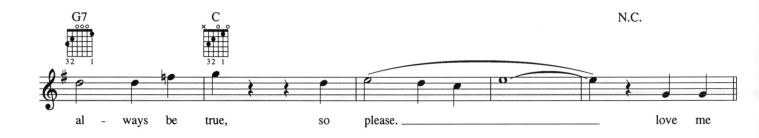

al - ways be true, so please. love me

Chorus

To Coda ⊕

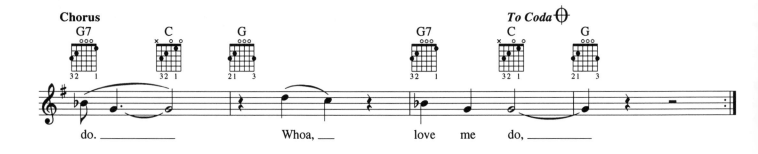

do. Whoa, love me do,

Bridge

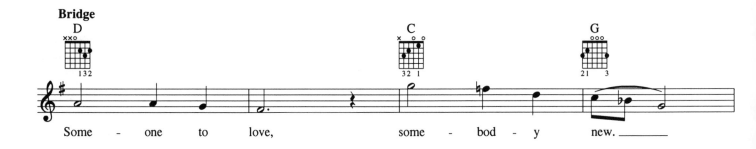

Some - one to love, some - bod - y new.

D.S. al Coda

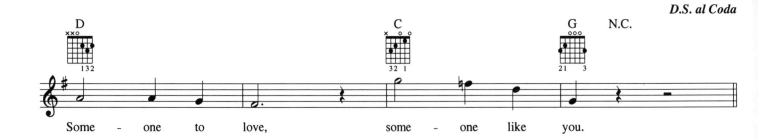

Some - one to love, some - one like you.

⊕ *Coda*

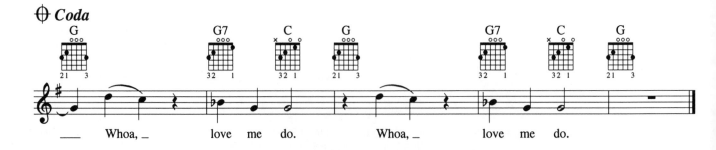

Whoa, love me do. Whoa, love me do.

Jingle Bells

Words and Music by J. Pierpont

Strum Pattern: 2, 3
Pick Pattern: 3, 4

Additional Lyrics

2. A day or two ago, I thought I'd take a ride,
   And soon Miss Fannie Bright was sitting by my side.
   The horse was lean and lank,
   Misfortune seemed his lot.
   He got into a drifted bank and we, we got upshot! Oh!

3. Now the ground is white, go it while you're young.
   Take the girls tonight and sing this sleighing song.
   Just get a bobtail bay,
   Two-forty for his speed.
   Then hitch him to an open sleigh and
   Crack, you'll take the lead! Oh

Maggie May

Words and Music by Rod Stewart and Martin Quittenton

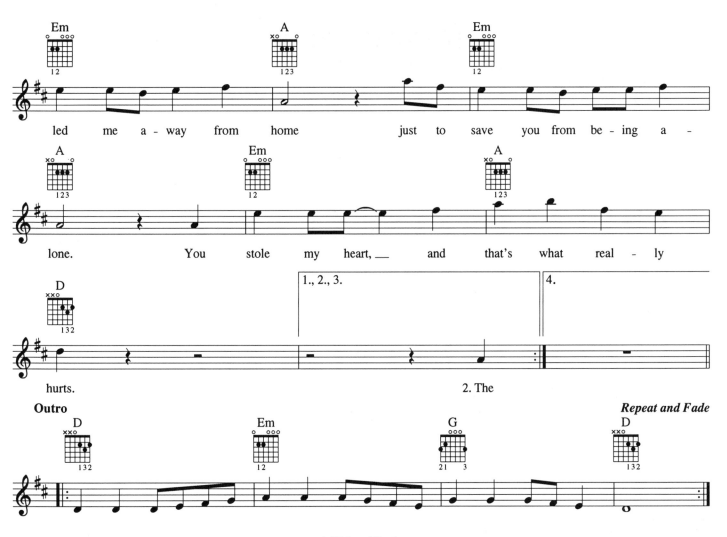

led me a-way from home   just to save you from be-ing a -

lone.   You stole my heart, ___ and that's what real-ly

1., 2., 3.   **4.**

hurts.   2. The

Outro   *Repeat and Fade*

Additional Lyrics

2. The morning sun, when it's in your face,
   Really shows your age.
   But that don't worry me none.
   In my eyes, you're everything.
   I laughed at all of your jokes.
   My love you didn't need to coax.
   Oh, Maggie, I couldn't have tried any more.
   You let me away from home
   Just to save you from being alone.
   You stole my soul, and that's a pain I can do without.

3. All I needed was a friend
   To lend a guiding hand.
   But you turned into a lover, and, mother, what a lover!
   You wore me out.
   All you did was wreck my bed,
   And, in the morning, kick me in the head.
   Oh, Maggie, I couldn't have tried any more.
   You led me away from home
   'Cause you didn't want to be alone.
   You stole my heart, I couldn't leave you if I tried.

4. I suppose I could collect my books
   And get on back to school.
   Or steal my daddy's cue
   And make a living out of playing pool.
   Or find myself a rock 'n' roll band
   That needs a helping hand.
   Oh, Maggie, I wish I'd never seen your face.
   You made a first-class fool out of me.
   But I'm as blind as a fool can be.
   You stole my heart, but I love you anyway.

Mercury Blues

Words and Music by Robert Geddins and K.C. Douglas

Strum Pattern: 1
Pick Pattern: 3

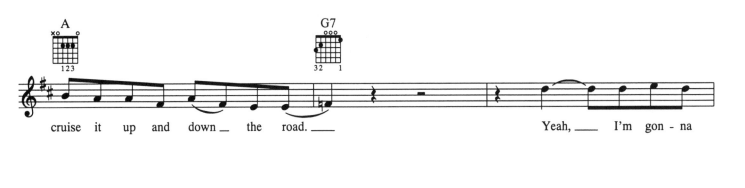

cruise it up and down __ the road. ____   Yeah, ____ I'm gon - na

buy __ me a Mer-cu - ry and cruise it up and down __ the road. __

Additional Lyrics

2. Well, the girl I love,
   I stole her from an friend.
   He got lucky, stole her back again.
   She heard he had a Mercury,
   Lord, she's crazy 'bout a Mercury.
   I'm gonna buy me a Mercury
   And cruise it up and down the road.

3. Well, hey now mama,
   You look so fine
   Ridin' 'round in your Mercury '49.
   Crazy 'bout a Mercury,
   Lord, I'm crazy 'bout a Mercury.
   I'm gonna buy me a Mercury
   And cruise it up and down the road.

4. Well, my baby went out,
   She didn't stay long.
   Bought herself a Mercury, come a cruisin' home.
   She's crazy 'bout a Mercury,
   Yeah, she's crazy 'bout a Mercury.
   I'm gonna buy me a Mercury
   And cruise it up and down the road.

My Generation

Words and Music by Peter Townshend

Strum Pattern: 4
Pick Pattern: 5

Verse

Fast Rock

1. Peo - ple try to put us down. Talk - in' 'bout my gen - er - a - tion.
2., 3. See Additional Lyrics

Just be-cause we get a - round. Talk - in' 'bout my gen - er - a - tion.

Things they do look aw - ful cold. Talk - in' 'bout my gen - er - a - tion.

Hope I die be - fore I get old. This is my gen - er -

Chorus

a - tion. __ This is my gen-er - a - tion, ba - by. ____

Additional Lyrics

2., 3. Why don't you all fade away? Talkin' 'bout my generation.
Don't try to dig what we all say. Talkin' 'bout my generation.
I'm not tryin' to cause a big sensation. Talkin' 'bout my generation.
I'm just talkin' 'bout my generation. Talkin' 'bout my generation.

My Girl

Words and Music by William "Smokey" Robinson and Ronald White

Strum Pattern: 2
Pick Pattern: 4

Additional Lyrics

2. I've got so much honey the bees envy me.
   I've got a sweeter song than the birds in the tree.

3. I don't need no money, fortune or fame.
   I've got all the riches, baby, one man can claim.

O Little Town Of Bethlehem

Traditional
Arranged for The King's Singers by Grayston Ives

Strum Pattern: 4
Pick Pattern: 5

Verse
Quietly

Additional Lyrics

2. For Christ is born of Mary, and gathered all above.
   While mortals sleep the angels keep
   Their watch of wond'ring love.
   O morning stars, together proclaim the holy birth!
   And praises sing to God the King,
   And peace to men on earth!

Rocky Mountain Way

Words and Music by Joe Walsh, Joe Vitale, Ken Passarelli and Rocke Grace

Strum Pattern: 1
Pick Pattern: 1

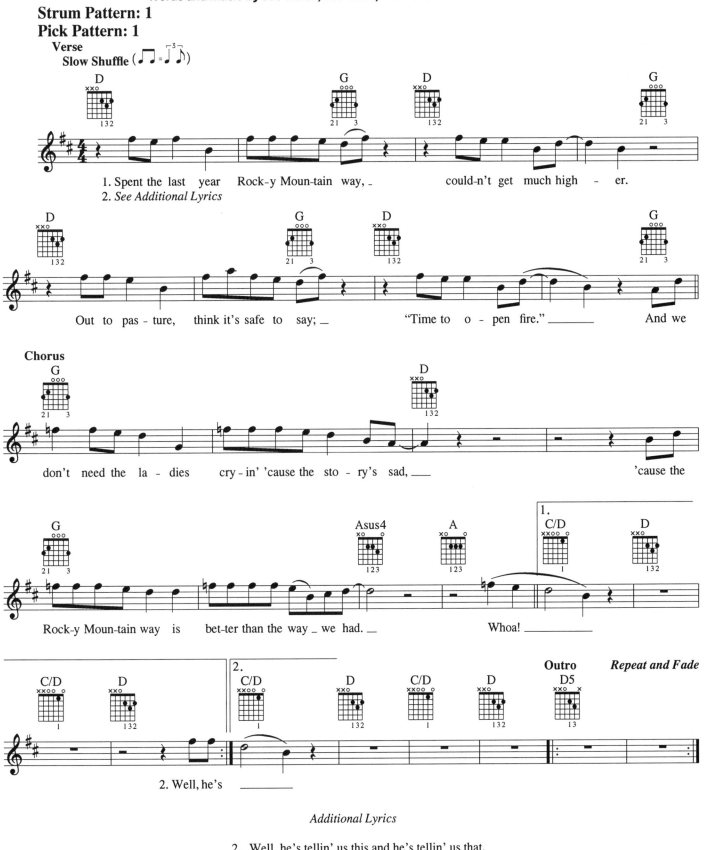

Additional Lyrics

2. Well, he's tellin' us this and he's tellin' us that,
   Changes it every day;
   Says it doesn't matter.
   Bases are loaded and Casey's at bat,
   Playin' it play by play;
   Time to change the batter.

MCA Music Publishing

Roxanne

Words and Music by Sting

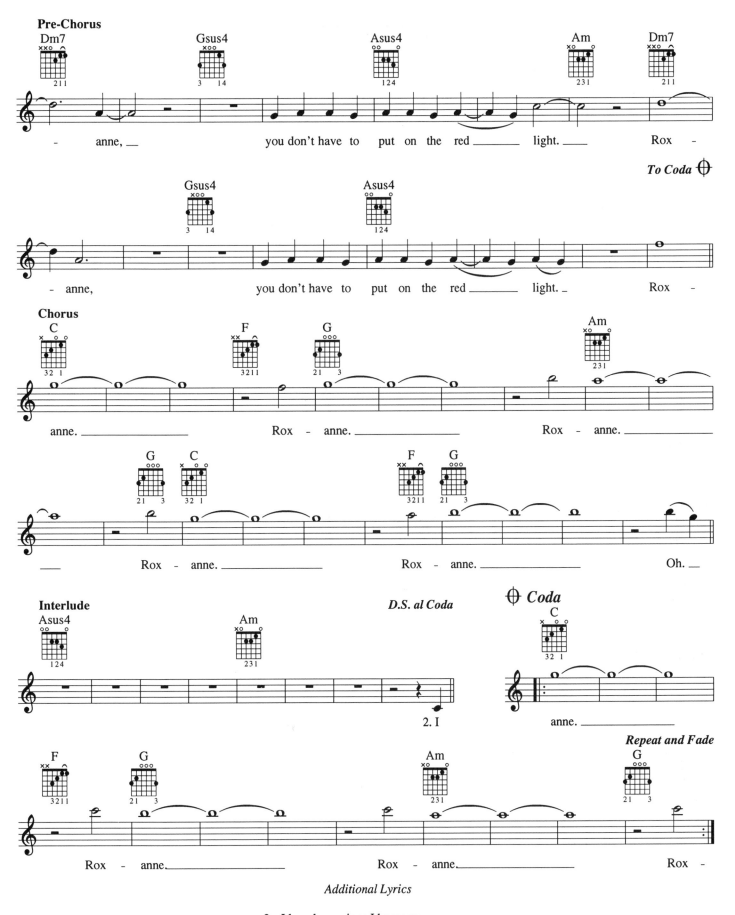

Additional Lyrics

2. I loved you since I knew ya.
   I wouldn't talk down to ya.
   I have to tell you just how I feel.
   I won't share you with another boy.
   I know my mind is made up.
   So put away your make-up.
   Told you once I won't tell you again.
   It's a crime the way...

Some Enchanted Evening

from SOUTH PACIFIC

Lyrics by Oscar Hammerstein II
Music by Richard Rodgers

Additional Lyrics

2. Some enchanted evening, someone maybe laughing,
   You may hear her laughing, across a crowded room.
   And night after night, as strange as it seems,
   The sound of her laughter will sing in your dreams.

The Sound of Music

from THE SOUND OF MUSIC
Lyrics by Oscar Hammerstein II
Music by Richard Rodgers

Strum Pattern: 4
Pick Pattern: 5

The Star Spangled Banner

Words by Francis Scott Key
Music by John Stafford Smith

Strum Pattern: 8
Pick Pattern: 8

Words by FRANCIS SCOTT KEY
Music by JOHN STAFFORD SMITH

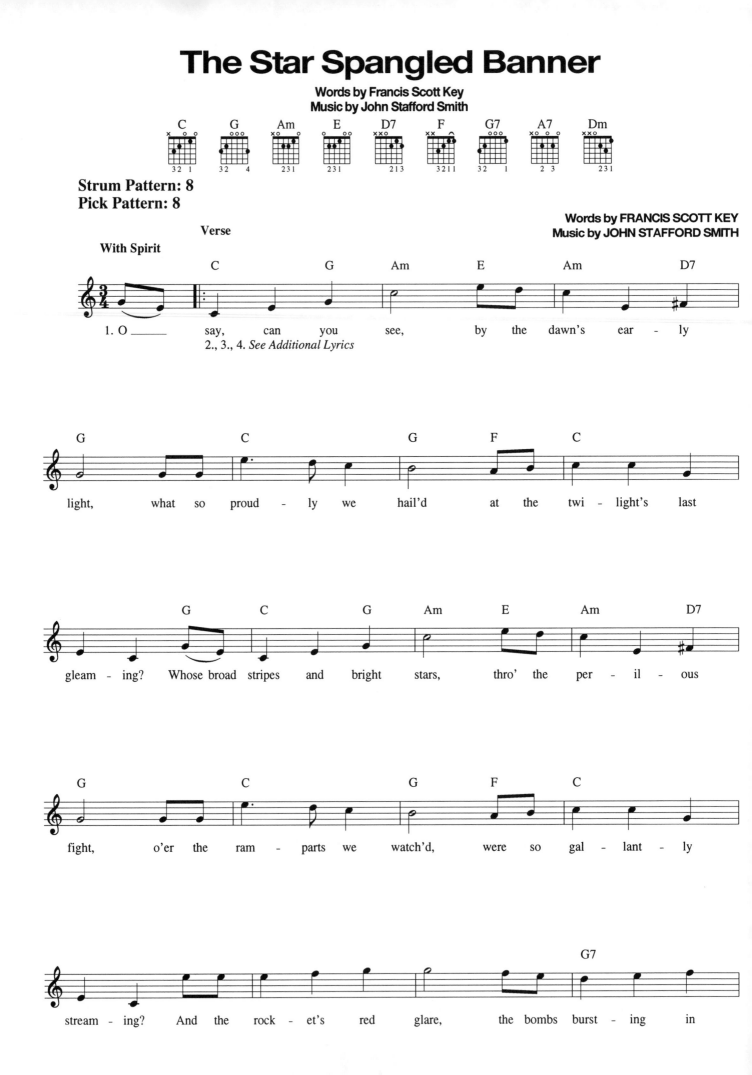

air gave proof thro' the night that our flag was still there. O

say, does that _____ star - span - gled ban - ner _____ yet _____ wave _____ o'er the

land _____ of the free and the home of the brave? On the brave.

Additional Lyrics

2. On the shore dimly seen thro' the mists of the deep,
   Where the foe's haughty host in dread silence reposes,
   What is that which the breeze, o'er the towering steep,
   As it fitfully blows, half conceals, half discloses?
   Now it catches the gleam of the morning's first beam,
   In full glory reflected now— shines in the stream.
   'Tis the star–spangled banner, o long may it wave
   O'er the land of the free and the home of the brave.

3. And where is the band who so dauntingly swore,
   'Mid the havoc of war and the battle's confusion.
   A home and a country they'd leave us no more?
   Their blood has wash'd out their foul footstep's pollution.
   No refuge could save the hireling and slave
   From the terror of flight or the gloom of the grave.
   And the star–spangled banner in triumph doth wave
   O'er the land of the free and the home of the brave.

4. O thus be it ever when free man shall stand,
   Between their loved homes and the war's desolation.
   Blest with vict'ry and peace, may the heav'n rescued land
   Praise the Power that hath made and preserved us a nation!
   Then conquer we must when our cause it is just,
   And this be our motto, "In God is our trust!"
   And the star–spangled banner in triumph shall wave
   O'er the land of the free and the home of the brave.

Takin' Care Of Business

Words and Music by Randy Bachman

Additional Lyrics

2. There's work easy as fishing,
   You could be a musician
   If you could make sounds loud and mellow.
   Get a second hand guitar,
   Chances are you'll go far
   If you get in with the right bunch of fellows.
   People see you having fun,
   Just a-lying in the sun.
   Tell them that you like it this way.
   It's the work that we avoid
   And we're all self-employed.
   We love to work at nothing all day.

We Will Rock You

Words and Music by Brian May

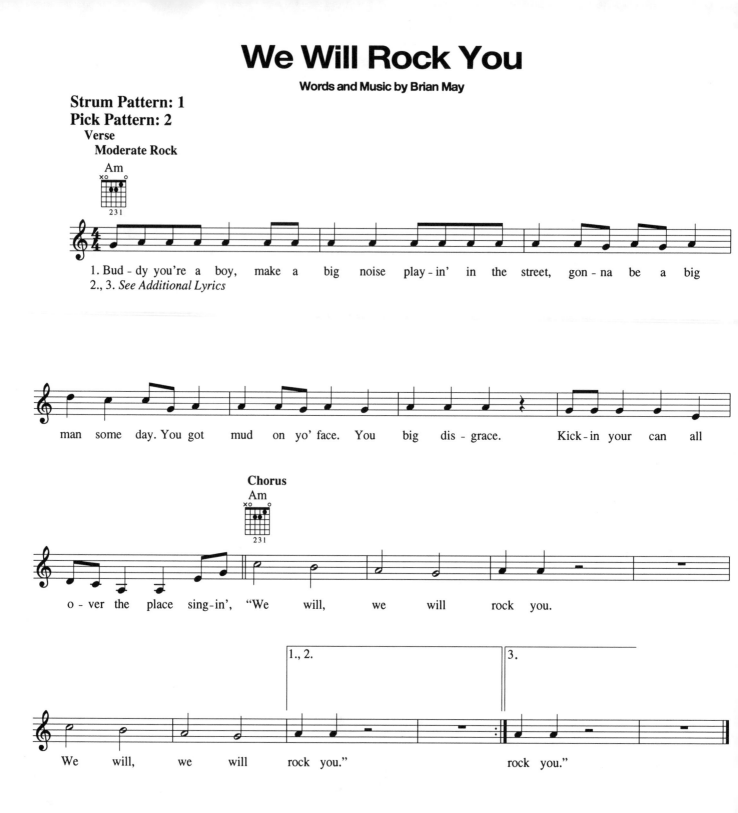

Strum Pattern: 1
Pick Pattern: 2

Verse
Moderate Rock

Am

1. Bud - dy you're a boy, make a big noise play-in' in the street, gon - na be a big
2., 3. *See Additional Lyrics*

man some day. You got mud on yo' face. You big dis - grace. Kick - in your can all

Chorus
Am

o - ver the place sing-in', "We will, we will rock you.

1., 2.   3.

We will, we will rock you."   rock you."

Additional Lyrics

2. Buddy you're a young man, hard man shoutin' in the street,
   Gonna take on the world some day.
   You got blood on yo' face.
   You big disgrace.
   Wavin' your banner all over the place singin',

3. Buddy you're an old man, poor man pleadin' with your eyes,
   Gonna make you some peace someday.
   You got mud on your face.
   You big disgrace.
   Somebody better put you back into your place singin',

T-R-O-U-B-L-E

Words and Music by Jerry Chesnut

Strum Pattern: 1
Pick Pattern: 2

Intro

Fast Rock

Well, ___ I play an old gui-tar ___ from nine 'till ___ half past one.

I'm just tryin' ___ to make a liv-ing, watch-ing ev-'ry-bod-y else hav-

ing fun.   Well, I don't miss much if it hap-pens on the dance hall

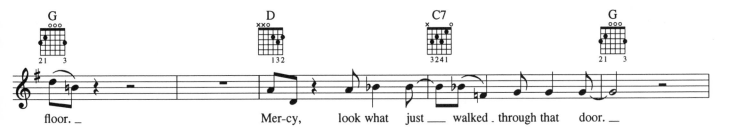

floor. ___   Mer-cy, look what just ___ walked through that door. ___

Chorus

Well, _____ hel-lo T-R-O-U-B-L-E,

tell me what in the world _ you do-in' A - L - O - N - E? ___

Yeah, ___ say hey ___ good L - dou-ble O - K - I - N - G. ___

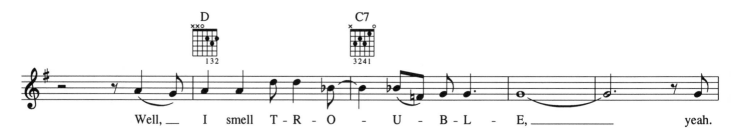
Well, __ I smell T - R - O - U - B - L - E, _____ yeah.

%⁉ **Verse**

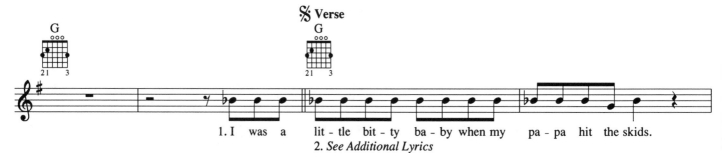
1. I was a lit - tle bit - ty ba - by when my pa - pa hit the skids.
2. *See Additional Lyrics*

Ma - ma had a time tryin' to raise nine kids. She told me not to stare 'cause it was

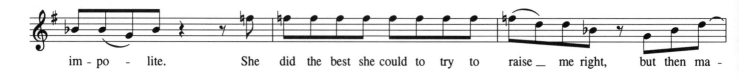
im - po - lite. She did the best she could to try to raise _ me right, but then ma -

- ma nev - er told me 'bout noth - in' like _ Y - O - U. Bet your ma -

178

Additional Lyrics

2. Well, you're a sweet talkin', sexy walkin', honky tonkin' baby.
   The men are gonna love you and the women gonna hate you,
   Reminding them of everything they're never gonna be.
   May be the beginning of a world war three,
   'Cause the world ain't ready for nothin' like you.
   I bet your mama must have been another good lookin' mama too.
   Yeah, hey good L-double O-K-I-N-G.
   Well, I smell T-R-O-U-B-L-E.

When the Saints Go Marching In

Words by Katherine E. Purvis
Music by James M. Black

Additional Lyrics

2. Oh, when the sun refuse to shine,
   Oh, when the sun refuse to shine,
   Oh Lord, I want to be in that number,
   When the sun refuse to shine.

3. Oh, when they crown Him Lord of all,
   Oh, when they crown Him Lord of all,
   Oh Lord, I want to be in that number,
   When they crown Him Lord of all.

4. Oh, when they gather 'round the throne,
   Oh, when they gather 'round the throne,
   Oh Lord, I want to be in that number,
   When they gather 'round the throne.

Wild Thing

Words and Music by Chip Taylor

Strum Pattern: 5
Pick Pattern: 1

You Needed Me

Words and Music by Randy Goodrum

Strum Pattern: 5
Pick Pattern: 2

Additional Lyrics

3. You held my hand, when it was cold.
   When I was lost, you took me home.
   You gave me hope, when I was at the end,
   And turned my lies back into truth again.
   You even called me friend.

Yankee Doodle

Traditional

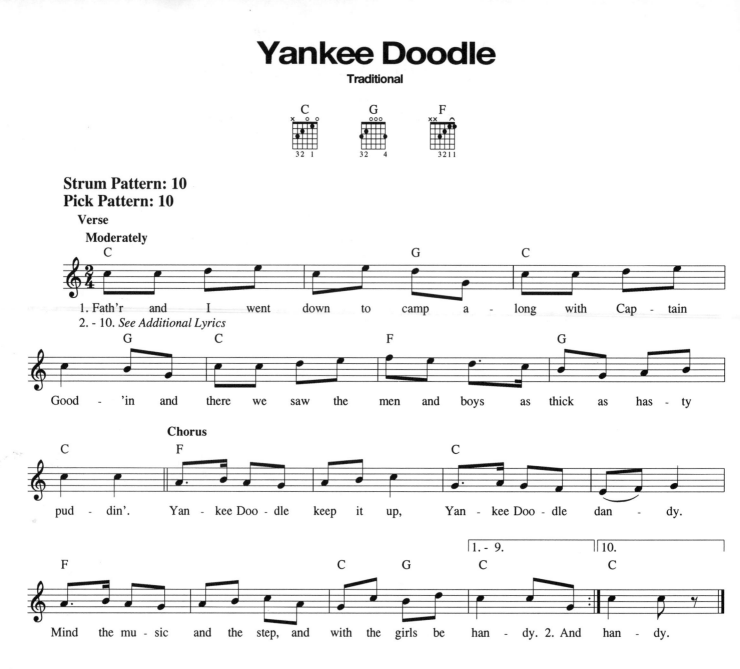

Strum Pattern: 10
Pick Pattern: 10

Verse
Moderately

1. Fath'r and I went down to camp a - long with Cap - tain
2. - 10. *See Additional Lyrics*

Good - 'in and there we saw the men and boys as thick as has - ty

Chorus

pud - din'. Yan - kee Doo - dle keep it up, Yan - kee Doo - dle dan - dy.

Mind the mu - sic and the step, and with the girls be han - dy. 2. And han - dy.

Additional Lyrics

2. And there we see a thousand men
   As rich as Squire David.
   And what they wasted ev'ry day
   I wish it could be saved.

3. And there was Captain Washington
   Upon a slapping stallion
   A-giving orders to his men,
   I guess there was a million.

4. And then the feathers on his hat,
   They looked so very fine, ah!
   I wanted peskily to get
   To give to my Jemima.

5. And there I see a swamping gun,
   Large as a log of maple,
   Upon a mighty little cart,
   A load for father's cattle.

6. And ev'ry time they fired it off,
   It took a horn of powder.
   It made a noise like father's gun,
   Only a nation louder.

7. An' there I see a little keg,
   Its head all made of leather.
   They knocked upon't with little sticks
   To call the folks together.

8. And Cap'n Davis had a gun,
   He kind o'clapt his hand on't
   And stuck a crooked stabbing-iron
   Upon the little end on't.

9. The troopers, too, would gallop up
   And fire right in ours faces.
   It scared me almost half to death
   To see them run such races.

10. It scared me so I hooked it off
    Nor stopped, as I remember,
    Nor turned about till I got home,
    Locked up in mother's chamber.

All the Things You Are

from VERY WARM FOR MAY
Lyrics by Oscar Hammerstein II
Music by Jerome Kern

Bridge

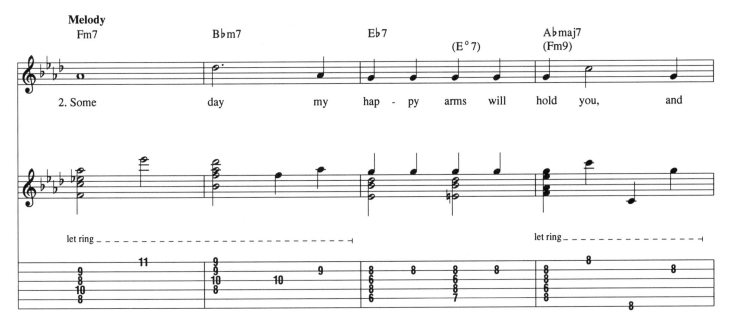

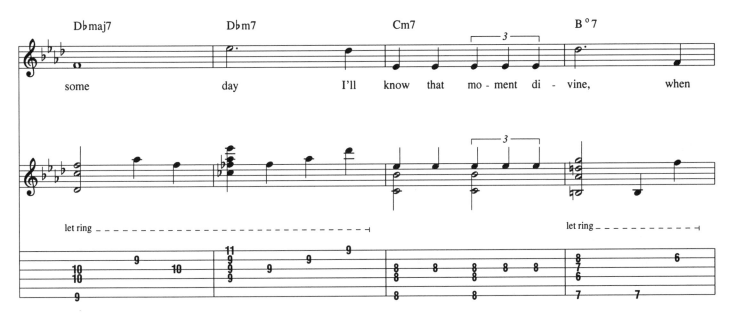

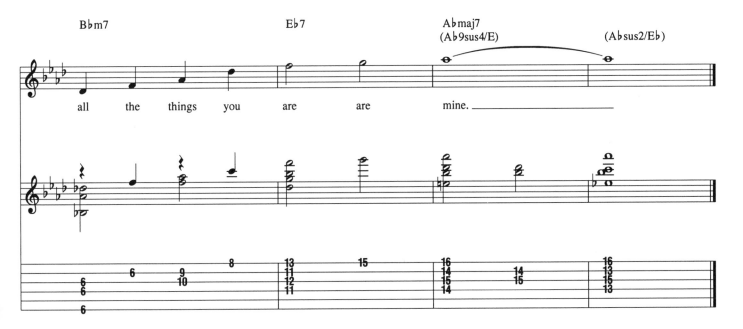

The Christmas Song

(Chestnuts Roasting on an Open Fire)
Music and Lyric by Mel Torme and Robert Wells

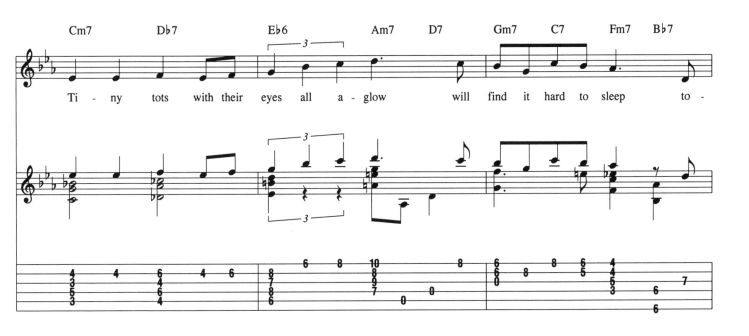

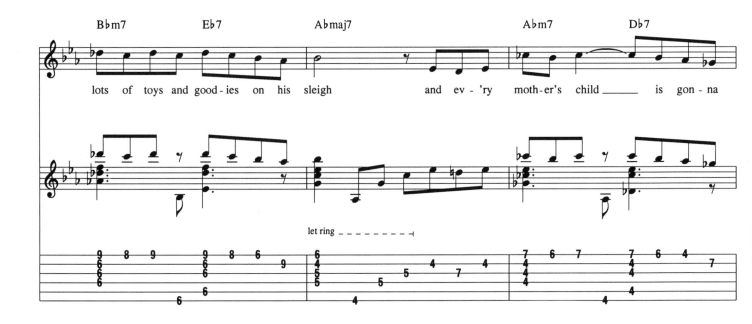

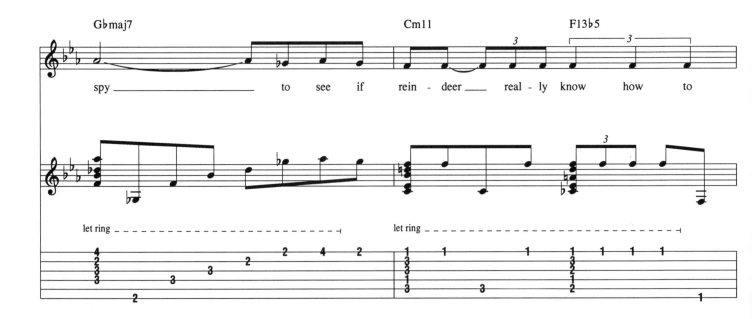

Misty

Words by Johnny Burke
Music by Erroll Garner

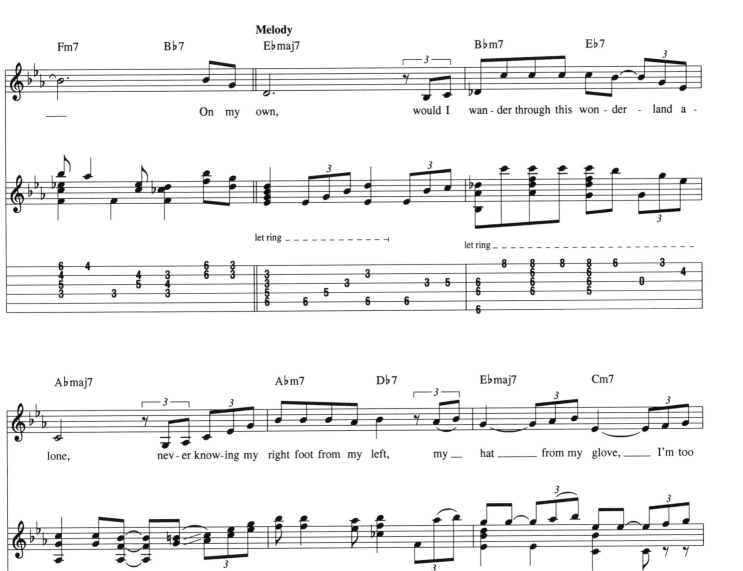

On my own, would I wan-der through this won-der-land a-

lone, nev-er know-ing my right foot from my left, my hat from my glove, I'm too

mis-ty and too much in love.

Stella by Starlight

from the Paramount Picture THE UNINVITED
Words by Ned Washington
Music by Victor Young

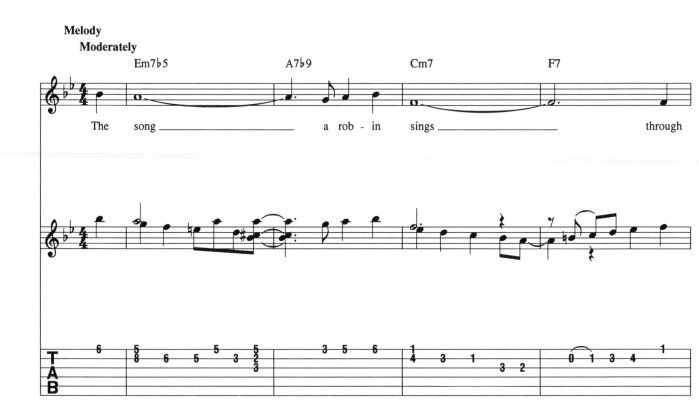

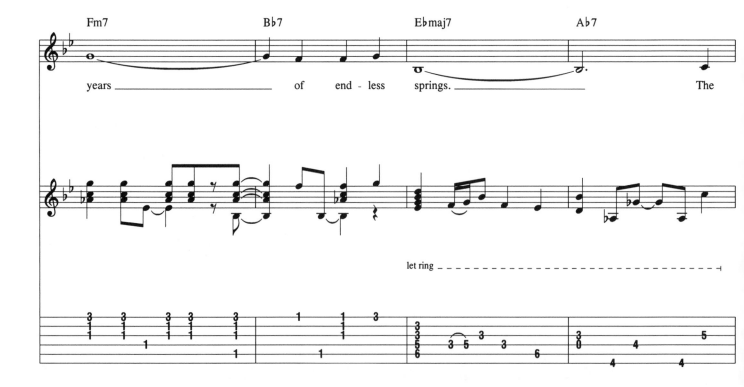

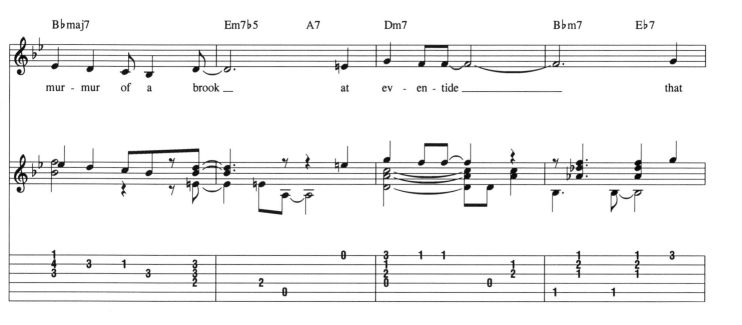

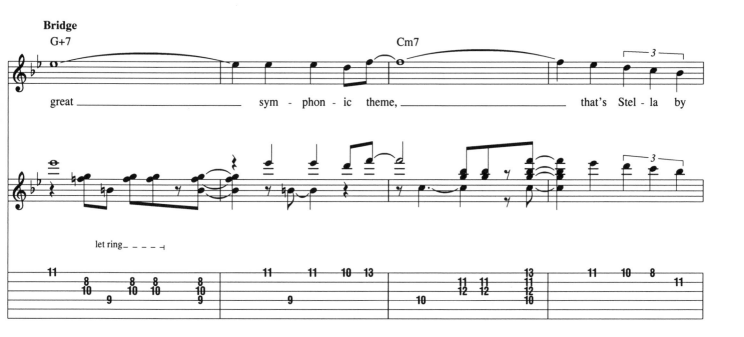

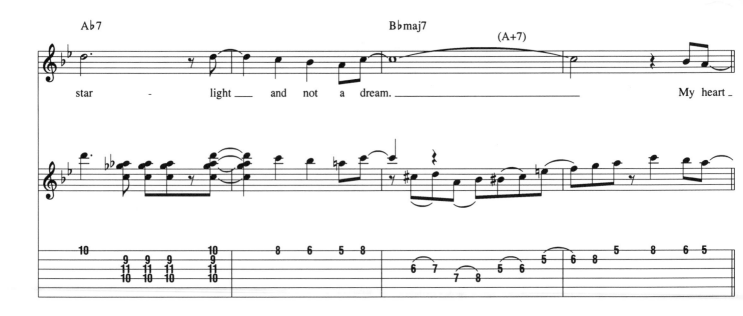

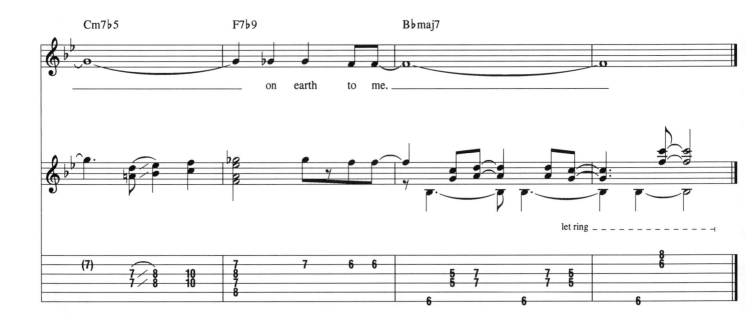

Minuet

By Robert de Visée

Estudio

By Dionisio Aguado

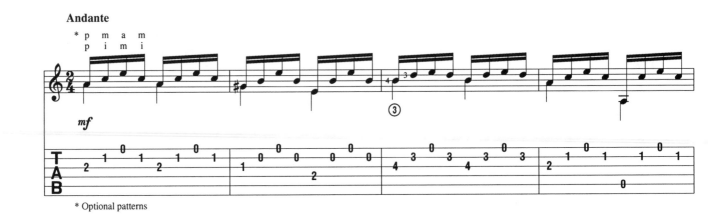

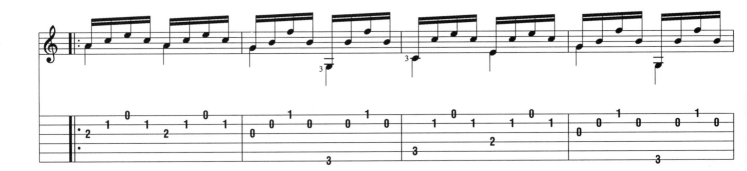

Bianco Fiore

Anonymous

Drop D Tuning:
①= E   ④= D
②= B   ⑤= A
③= G   ⑥= D

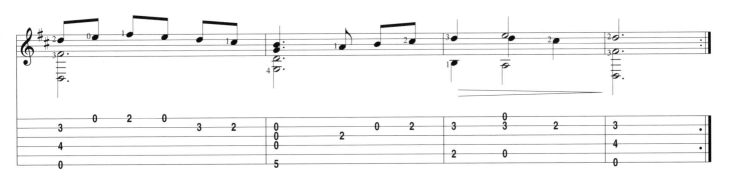

Estudio

By Fernando Sor

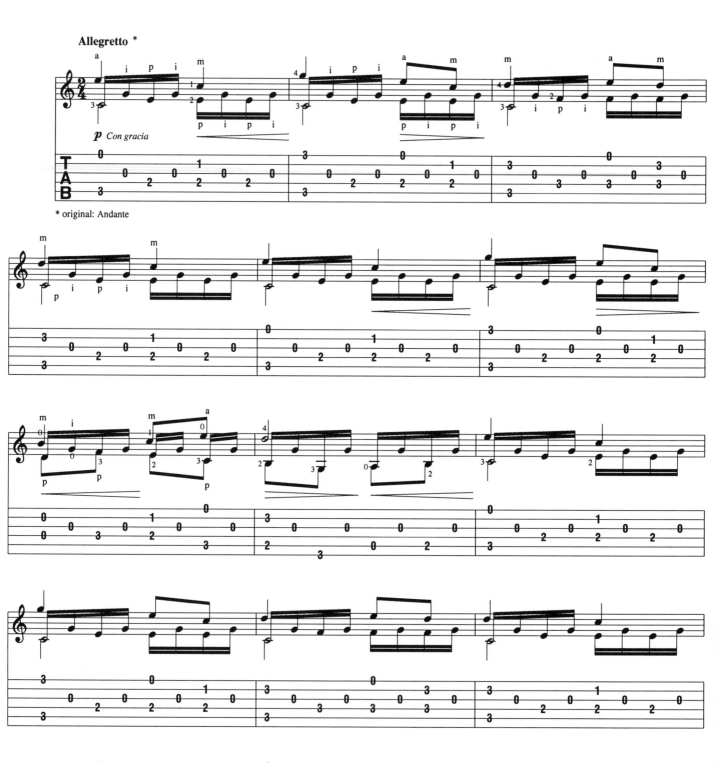

* original: Andante

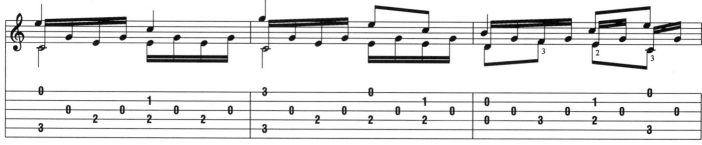

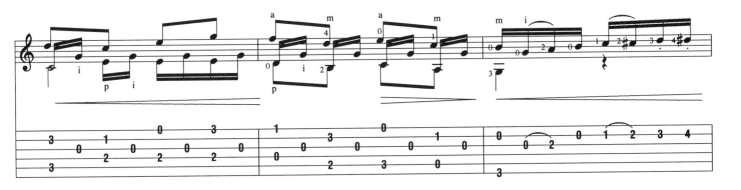

Lagrima

By Francisco Tárrega

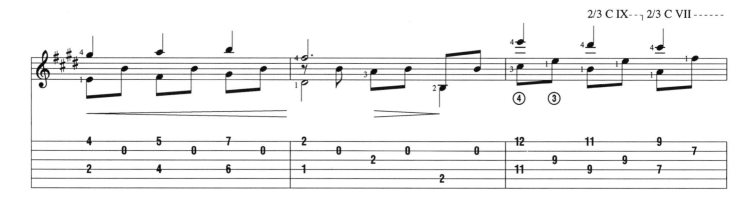

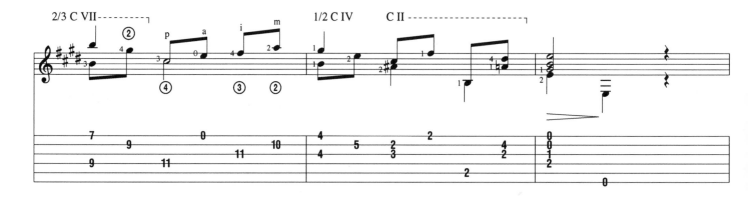

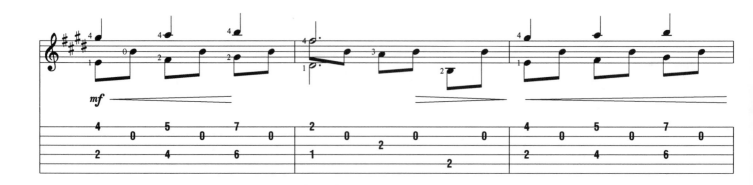

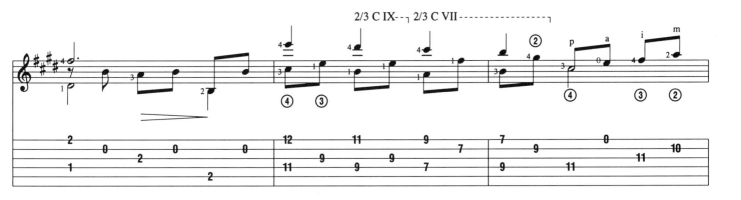

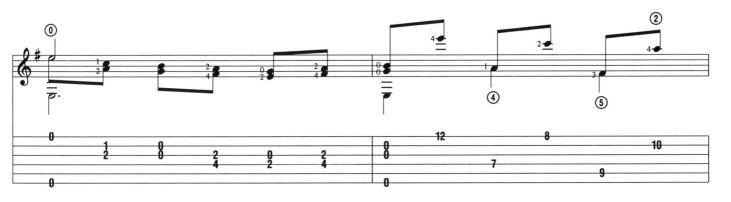

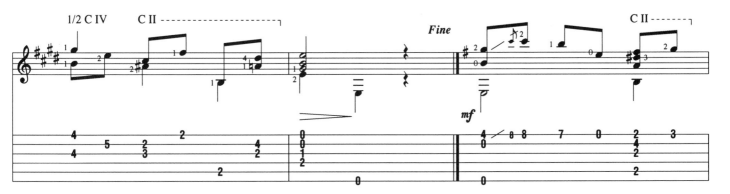

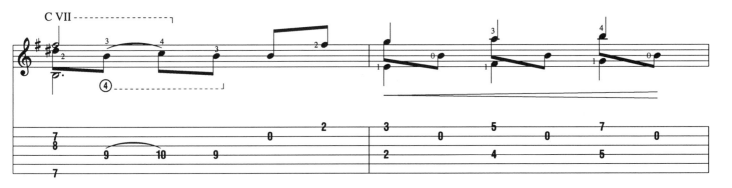

Minuet

By Johann Krieger

Moderato ♩ = 108

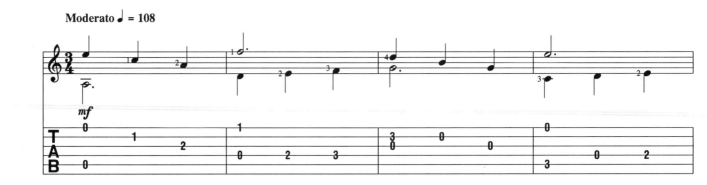

Fine

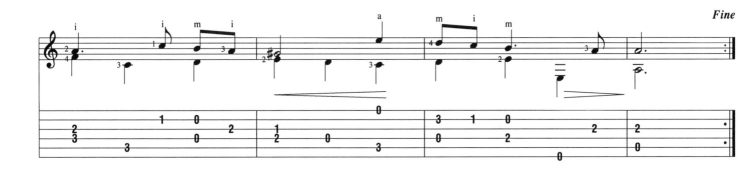

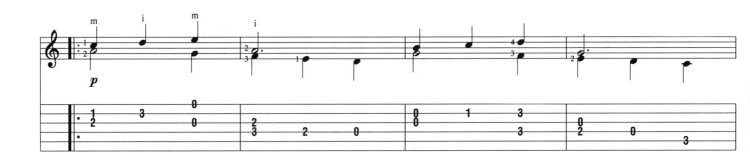

D.C. al Fine

Pavane

Anonymous

Adagio ♩ = 80

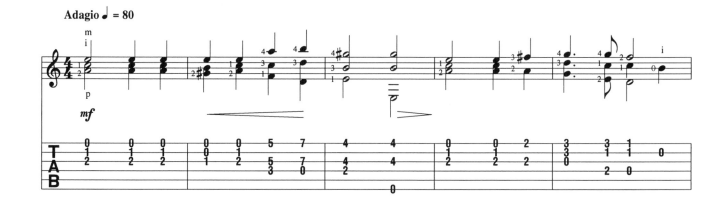

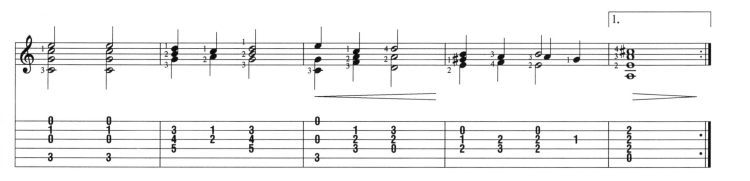

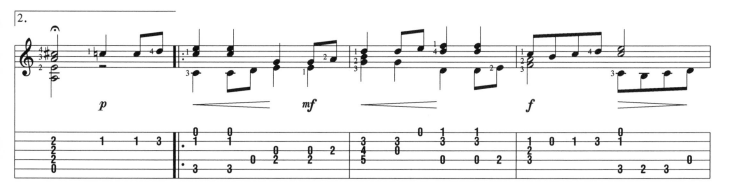

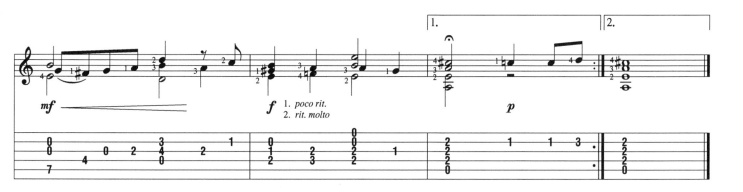

Bury Me Not on the Lone Prairie

Words based on the poem "The Ocean Burial" by Rev. Edwin H. Chapin
Music by Ossain N. Dodge

Additional Lyrics

2. "Oh, bury me not on the lone prairie,
   Where the wild coyotes will howl o'er me,
   In a narrow grave just six by three.
   Oh, bury me not on the lone prairie."

3. "It matters not, I've oft been told,
   Where the body lies when the heart grows cold.
   Yet grant, oh grant this wish to me:
   Oh, bury me not on the lone prairie."

5. "Oh, bury me not" - and his voice failed there,
   But we took no heed of his dying prayer.
   In a narrow grave just six by three
   We buried him there on the lone prairie.

4. "I've always wished to be laid where I died
   In the little churchyard on the green hillside.
   By my father's grave, there let mine be
   And bury me not on the lone prairie."

6. And the cowboys now as they roam the plain,
   For they marked the spot where his bones were lain,
   Fling a handful of roses o'er his grave
   With a prayer to Him who his soul will save.

Scarborough Fair

Traditional English

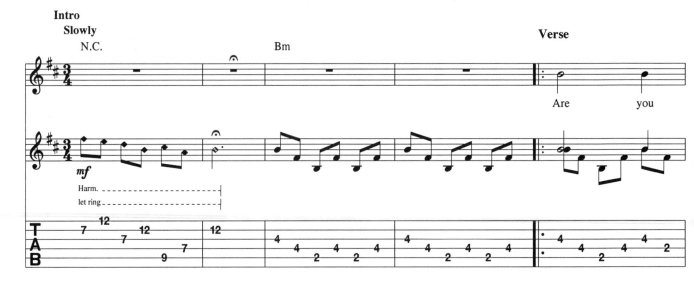

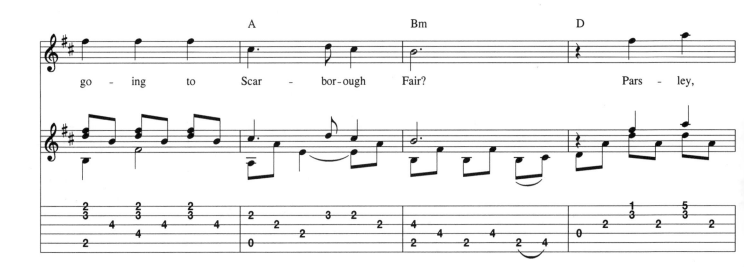

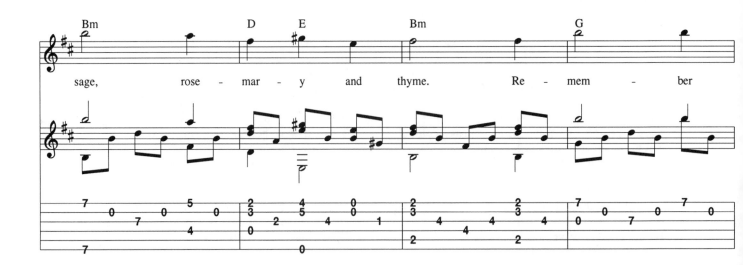

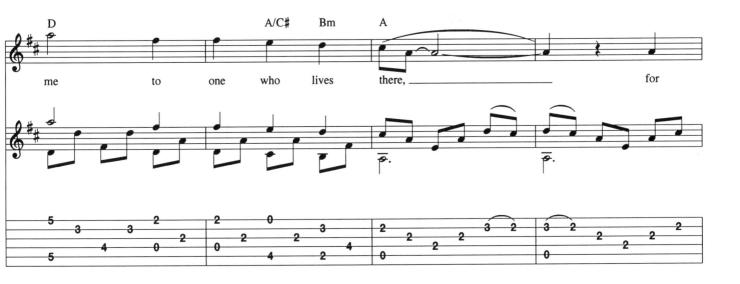

me   to   one   who   lives   there,   for

once   she   was   a   true   love   of   mine.

mine.

My Funny Valentine

from BABES IN ARMS

Words by Lorenz Hart
Music by Richard Rodgers

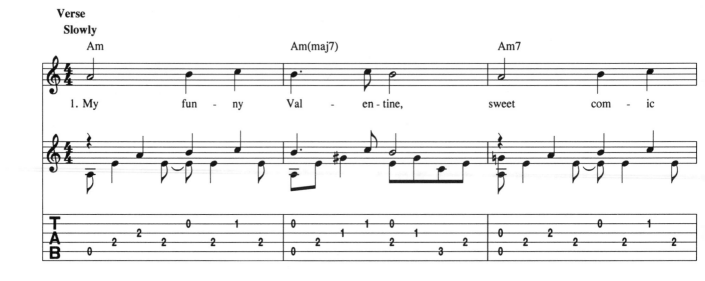

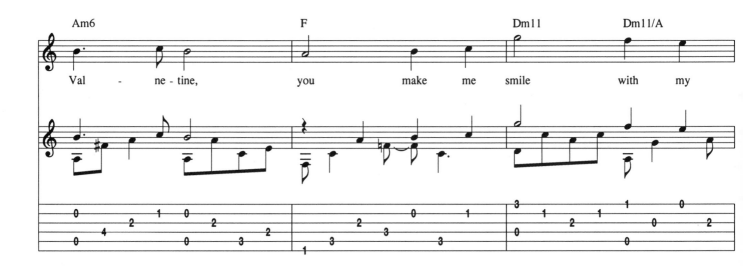

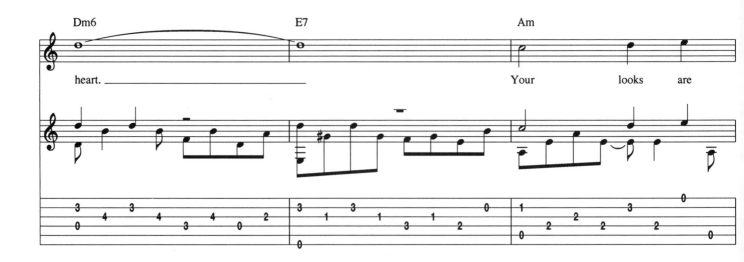

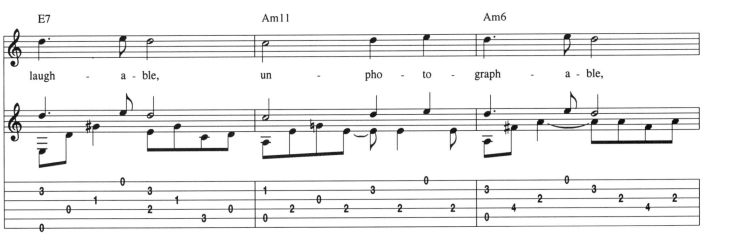

laugh - a - ble, un - pho - to - graph - a - ble,

yet, you're my fav - 'rite work of art. _____

Bridge

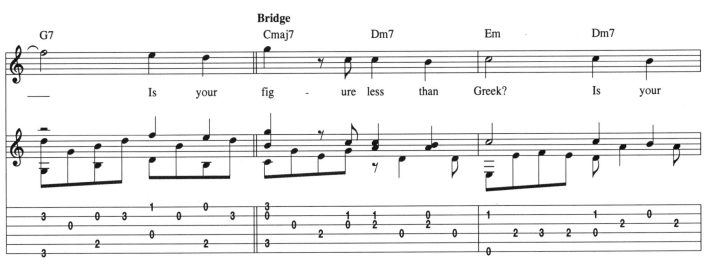

Is your fig - ure less than Greek? Is your

mouth a lit - tle weak, when you o - pen it to speak are you

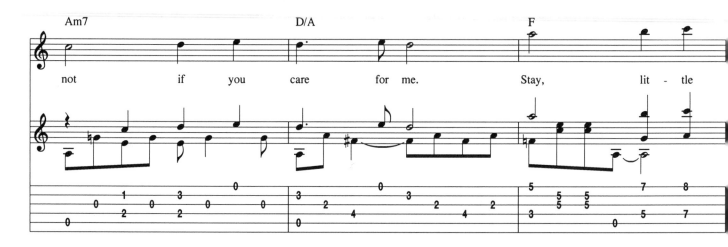

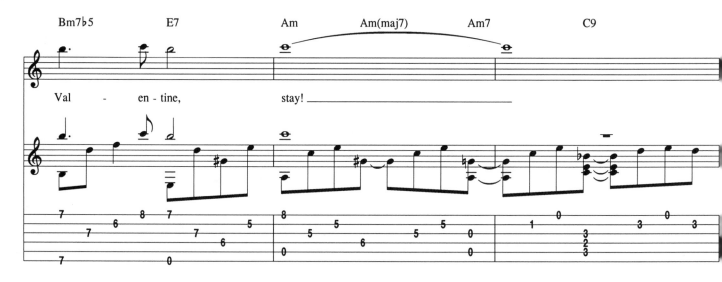

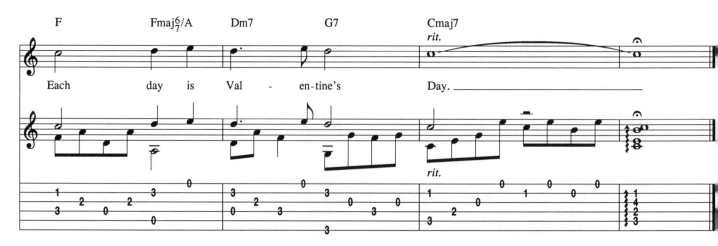

Shenandoah

American Folksong

Tears In Heaven

Words and Music by Eric Clapton and Will Jennings

A Whole New World
(Aladdin's Theme)

from Walt Disney's ALADDIN

Music by Alan Menken
Lyrics by Tim Rice

Drop D Tuning:
①=E ④=D
②=B ⑤=A
③=G ⑥=D

Intro
Slowly

Verse

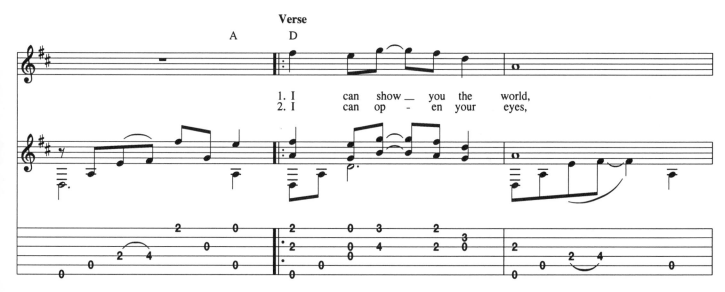

1. I can show __ you the world,
2. I can op - en your eyes,

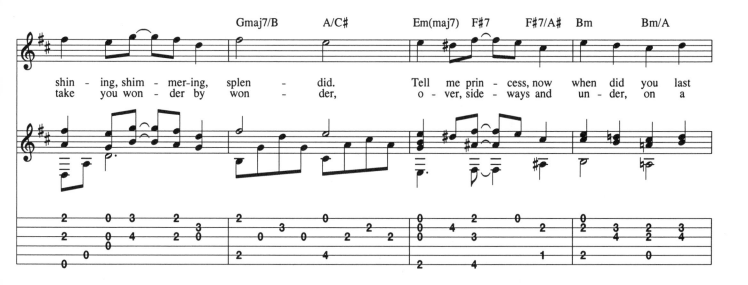

shin - ing, shim - mer-ing, splen - did. Tell me prin - cess, now when did you last
take you won - der by won - der, o - ver, side - ways and un - der, on a

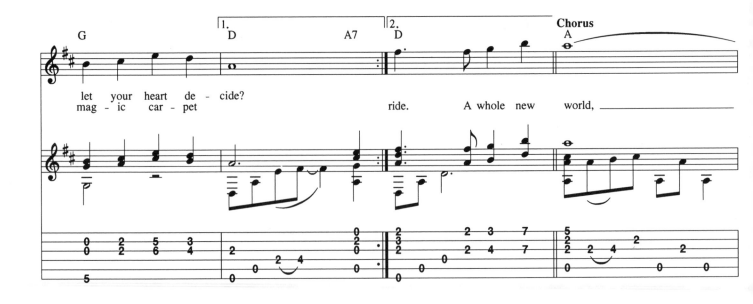

let your heart de - cide?
mag - ic car - pet ride.   A whole new world,_____

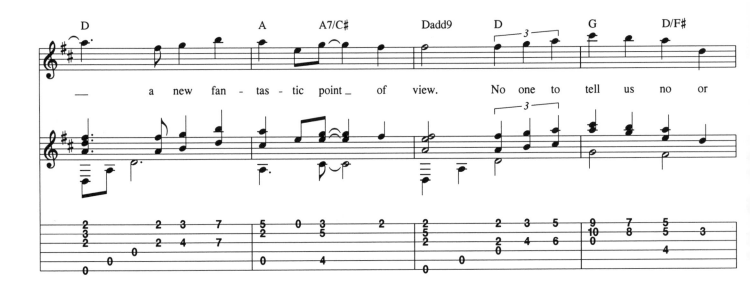

____ a new fan - tas - tic point __ of view.   No one to tell us no or

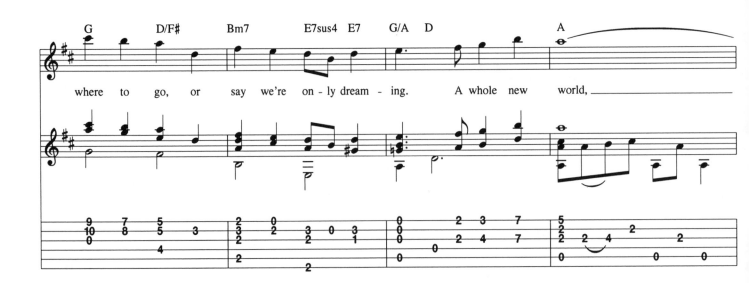

where to go,   or   say we're on - ly dream - ing.   A whole new world,_____

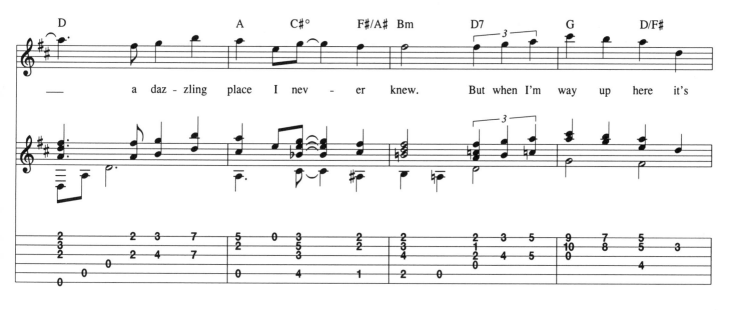

a daz - zling place I nev - er knew. But when I'm way up here it's

crys - tal clear that now I'm in a whole new world with you.

All Day And All Of The Night

Words and Music by Ray Davies

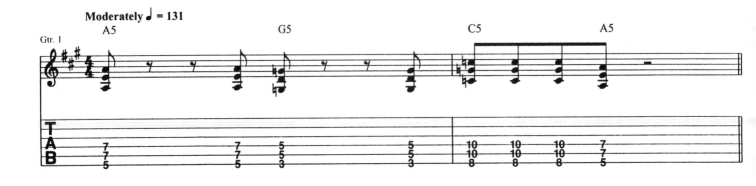

All Right Now

Words and Music by Paul Rodgers and Andy Fraser

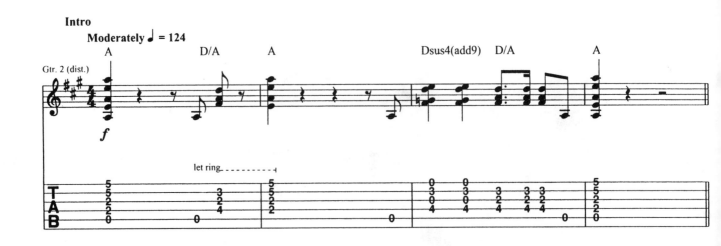

Crazy Train

Words and Music by Ozzy Osbourne, Randy Rhoads and Bob Daisley

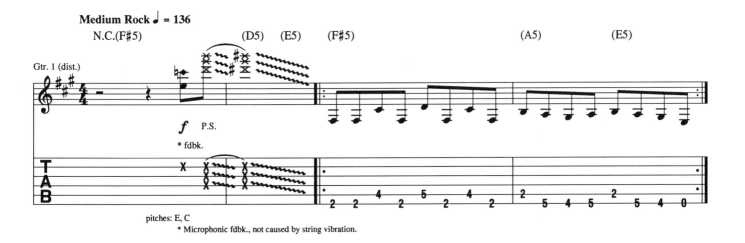

pitches: E, C

* Microphonic fdbk., not caused by string vibration.

Cult of Personality

**Words and Music by William Calhoun, Corey Glover,
Muzz Skillings, and Vernon Reid**

Day Tripper

Words and Music by John Lennon and Paul McCartney

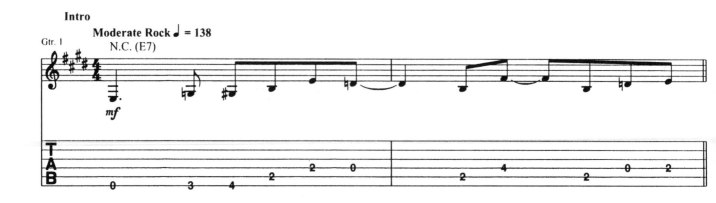

Deuce

Words and Music by Gene Simmons

I Feel Fine

Words and Music by John Lennon and Paul McCartney

I'll Stick Around

Words and Music by David Grohl

I'm Your Hoochie Coochie Man

Written by Willie Dixon

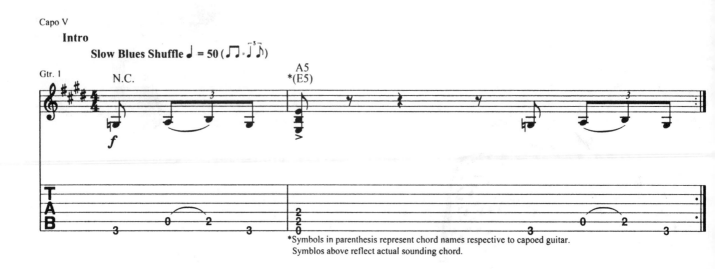

*Symbols in parenthesis represent chord names respective to capoed guitar.
Symblos above reflect actual sounding chord.

Iron Man

Words and Music by Frank Iommi, John Osbourne, William Ward and Terence Butler

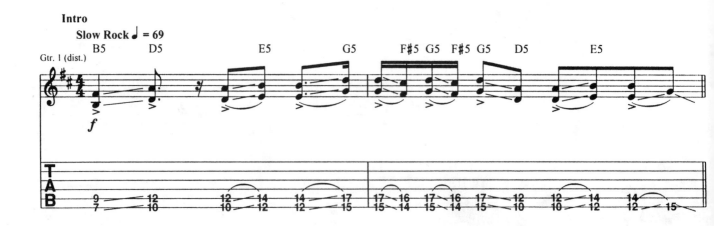

Message In A Bottle

Words and Music by Sting

Money

Words and Music by Roger Waters

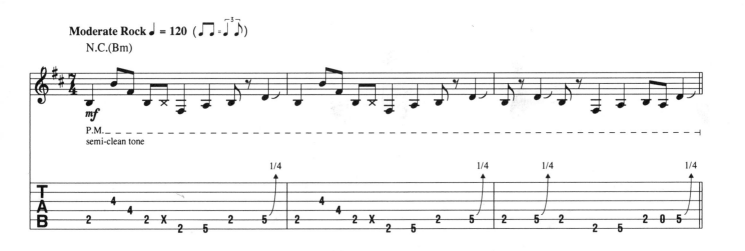

More Than a Feeling

Words and Music by Tom Scholz

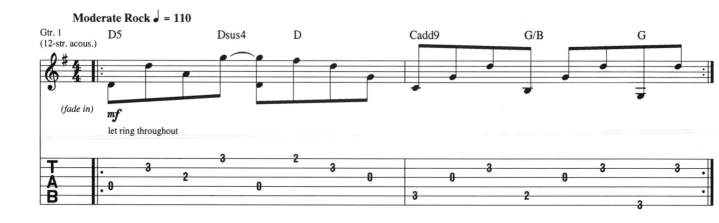

Moderate Rock ♩ = 110

Name

Words and Music by John Rzeznik

Tuning:
①= E ④= E
②= E ⑤= A
③= A ⑥= D

Moderately Fast Half-Time Feel ♩ = 148

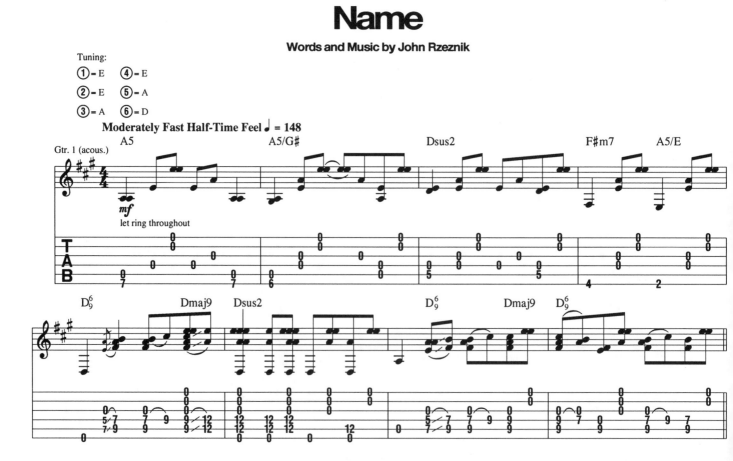

Oh, Pretty Woman

Words and Music by Roy Orbison and Bill Dees

Paperback Writer

Words and Music by John Lennon and Paul McCartney

Smoke on the Water

Words and Music by Ritchie Blackmore, Ian Gillan, Roger Glover, Jon Lord and Ian Paice

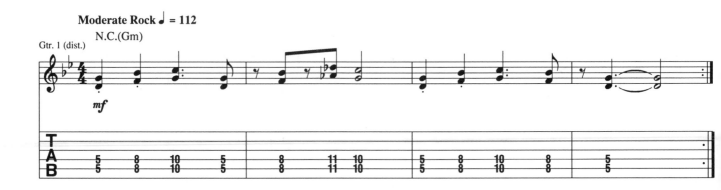

Start Me Up

Words and Music by Mick Jagger and Keith Richards

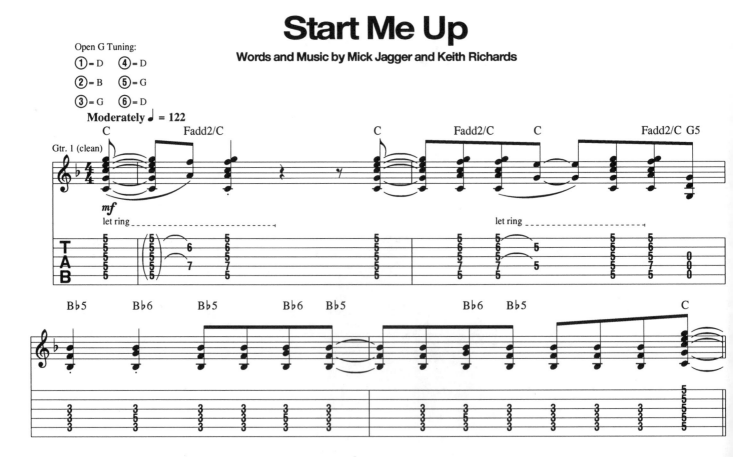

Substitute

Words and Music by Peter Townshend

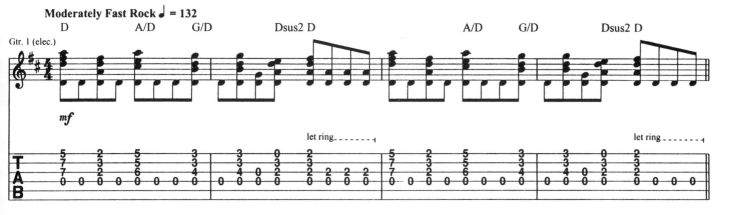

Sunshine Of Your Love

Words and Music by Jack Bruce, Pete Brown and Eric Clapton

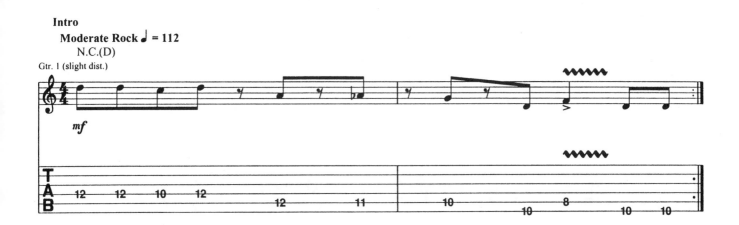

Sweet Home Alabama

Words and Music by Ronnie Van Zant, Ed King and Gary Rossington

Walk This Way

Words and Music Steven Tyler and Joe Perry

STRUM AND PICK PATTERNS

This chart contains the suggested strum and pick patterns that are referred to by number at the beginning
of each song in this book. The symbols ⊓ and ∨ in the strum patterns refer to down and up strokes, respectively.
The letters in the pick patterns indicate which right-hand fingers plays which strings.

p = thumb
i = index finger
m = middle finger
a = ring finger

For example; Pick Pattern 2
is played: thumb - index - middle - ring

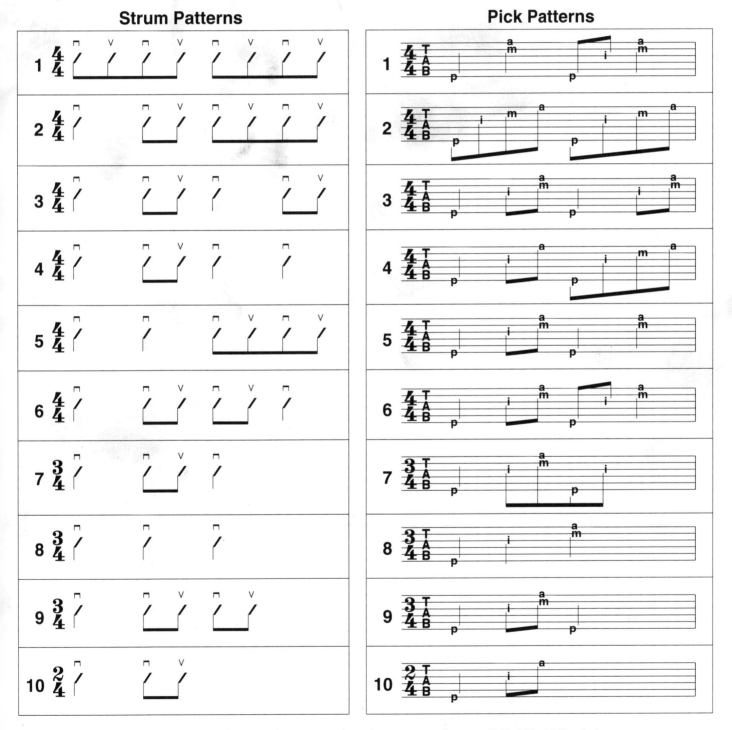

Strum Patterns   **Pick Patterns**

You can use the 3/4 Strum or Pick Patterns in songs written in compound meter (6/8, 9/8, 12/8, etc.).
For example, you can accompany a song in 6/8 by playing the 3/4 pattern twice in each measure.
The 4/4 Strum and Pick Patterns can be used for songs written in cut time (¢) by doubling the note
time values in the patterns. Each pattern would therefore last two measures in cut time.

Guitar Notation Legend

Guitar Music can be notated three different ways: on a *musical staff*, in *tablature*, and in *rhythm slashes*.

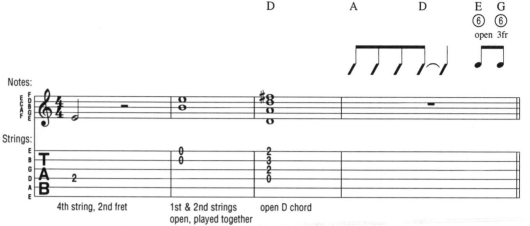

RHYTHM SLASHES are written above the staff. Strum chords in the rhythm indicated. Use the chord diagrams found at the top of the first page of the transcription for the appropriate chord voicings. Round noteheads indicate single notes.

THE MUSICAL STAFF shows pitches and rhythms and is divided by bar lines into measures. Pitches are named after the first seven letters of the alphabet.

TABLATURE graphically represents the guitar fingerboard. Each horizontal line represents a a string, and each number represents a fret.

4th string, 2nd fret

1st & 2nd strings open, played together

open D chord

Definitions for Special Guitar Notation

HALF-STEP BEND: Strike the note and bend up 1/2 step.

WHOLE-STEP BEND: Strike the note and bend up one step.

GRACE NOTE BEND: Strike the note and bend up as indicated. The first note does not take up any time.

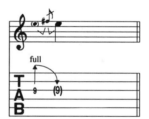

SLIGHT (MICROTONE) BEND: Strike the note and bend up 1/4 step.

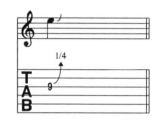

BEND AND RELEASE: Strike the note and bend up as indicated, then release back to the original note. Only the first note is struck.

PRE-BEND: Bend the note as indicated, then strike it.

PRE-BEND AND RELEASE: Bend the note as indicated. Strike it and release the bend back to the original note.

UNISON BEND: Strike the two notes simultaneously and bend the lower note up to the pitch of the higher.

VIBRATO: The string is vibrated by rapidly bending and releasing the note with the fretting hand.

WIDE VIBRATO: The pitch is varied to a greater degree by vibrating with the fretting hand.

HAMMER-ON: Strike the first (lower) note with one finger, then sound the higher note (on the same string) with another finger by fretting it without picking.

PULL-OFF: Place both fingers on the notes to be sounded. Strike the first note and without picking, pull the finger off to sound the second (lower) note.

LEGATO SLIDE: Strike the first note and then slide the same fret-hand finger up or down to the second note. The second note is not struck.

SHIFT SLIDE: Same as legato slide, except the second note is struck.

TRILL: Very rapidly alternate between the notes indicated by continuously hammering on and pulling off.

TAPPING: Hammer ("tap") the fret indicated with the pick-hand index or middle finger and pull off to the note fretted by the fret hand.

NATURAL HARMONIC: Strike the note while the fret-hand lightly touches the string directly over the fret indicated.

PINCH HARMONIC: The note is fretted normally and a harmonic is produced by adding the edge of the thumb or the tip of the index finger of the pick hand to the normal pick attack.

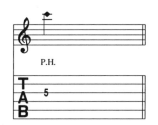

HARP HARMONIC: The note is fretted normally and a harmonic is produced by gently resting the pick hand's index finger directly above the indicated fret (in parentheses) while the pick hand's thumb or pick assists by plucking the appropriate string.

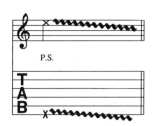

PICK SCRAPE: The edge of the pick is rubbed down (or up) the string, producing a scratchy sound.

MUFFLED STRINGS: A percussive sound is produced by laying the fret hand across the string(s) without depressing, and striking them with the pick hand.

PALM MUTING: The note is partially muted by the pick hand lightly touching the string(s) just before the bridge.

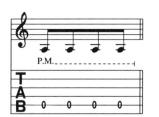

RAKE: Drag the pick across the strings indicated with a single motion.

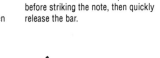

TREMOLO PICKING: The note is picked as rapidly and continuously as possible.

ARPEGGIATE: Play the notes of the chord indicated by quickly rolling them from bottom to top.

VIBRATO BAR DIVE AND RETURN: The pitch of the note or chord is dropped a specified number of steps (in rhythm) then returned to the original pitch.

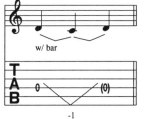

VIBRATO BAR SCOOP: Depress the bar just before striking the note, then quickly release the bar.

VIBRATO BAR DIP: Strike the note and then immediately drop a specified number of steps, then release back to the original pitch.

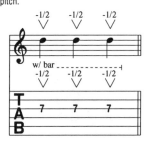

Additional Musical Definitions

(accent)	• Accentuate note (play it louder)	
(accent)	• Accentuate note with great intensity	
(staccato)	• Play the note short	
⊓	• Downstroke	
∨	• Upstroke	

Rhy. Fig. • Label used to recall a recurring accompaniment pattern (usually chordal).

Riff • Label used to recall composed, melodic lines (usually single notes) which recur.

Fill • Label used to identify a brief melodic figure which is to be inserted into the arrangement.

Rhy. Fill • A chordal version of a Fill.

tacet • Instrument is silent (drops out).

D.S. al Coda • Go back to the sign (𝄋), then play until the measure marked "**To Coda**," then skip to the section labelled "**Coda**."

D.S. al Fine • Go back to the beginning of the song and play until the measure marked "**Fine**" (end).

• Repeat measures between signs.

1.	2.

• When a repeated section has different endings, play the first ending only the first time and the second ending only the second time.

NOTE: Tablature numbers in parentheses mean:
1. The note is being sustained over a system (note in standard notation is tied), or
2. The note is sustained, but a new articulation (such as a hammer-on, pull-off, slide or vibrato begins, or
3. The note is a barely audible "ghost" note (note in standard notation is also in parentheses).

THE GUITAR TECHNIQUES SERIES

The series designed to get you started! Each book clearly presents essential concepts, highlighting specific elements of guitar playing and music theory. Most books include tablature and standard notation.

Acoustic Rock For Guitar

The acoustic guitar has found renewed popularity in contemporary rock. From ballads to metal, you'll find many artists adding that distinctive acoustic sound to their songs. This book demonstrates the elements of good acoustic guitar playing – both pick and fingerstyle – that are used in rock today. Topics include Chords and Variations, Strumming Styles, Picking Patterns, Scales and Runs, and much more.
00699327......................................$6.95

Arpeggios For Guitar

An introduction to the basics, including: Performance etudes; one-octave arpeggios; five-and six-string forms; string-skipping forms; and more.
00695044 ....$6.95

Basic Blues For Guitar

This book taps into the history of great blues guitarists like B.B. King and Muddy Waters. It teaches the guitarist blues accompaniments, bar chords and how to improvise leads.
00699008 ....$6.95

Music Theory For Guitar

Music theory is the cornerstone in understanding music. But how does a guitar player relate it to the guitar? This volume answers that question. Concepts of scale, harmony, chords, intervals and modes are presented in the context of applying them to the guitar. This book will open the door to not only understanding the fundamentals of music, but also the world of playing the guitar with more insight and intelligence.
00699329......................................$7.95

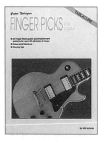

Finger Picks For Guitar

A convenient reference to 47 fingerstyle guitar accompaniment patterns for use with all types of music. In standard notation and tablature. Also includes playing tips.
00699125 ....$6.95

Lead Blues Licks

This book examines a number of blues licks in the styles of such greats as B.B. King, Albert King, Stevie Ray Vaughan, Eric Clapton, Chuck Berry, and more. Varying these licks and combining them with others can improve lead playing and can be used in rock styles as well as blues. Clearly written in notes and tab, you'll progress from the standard blues progression and blues scale to the various techniques of bending, fast pull offs and hammer-ons, double stops, and more.
00699325......................................$6.95

Lead Rock Licks For Guitar

Learn the latest hot licks played by great guitarists, including Jeff Beck, Neal Schon (of Journey), Andy Summers (Police), and Randy Rhoads (Ozzy Osbourne). The guitarist can use each lick in this book as building material to further create new and more exciting licks of their own.
00699007 ....$6.95

Rhythms For Blues For Guitar

This book brings to life everything you need to play blues rhythm patterns, in a quick, handy and easy-to-use book. Everything from basic blues progressions to turnarounds, including swing, shuffle, straight eighths rhythms, plus small, altered and sliding chord patterns. All are presented in the style of many of the great blues and rock blues legends. Includes notes and tab.
00699326......................................$6.95

Extended Scale Playing For Guitar

An innovative approach to expanding left hand technique by Joe Puma. The sliding first finger technique presented in this book will give players a new and broader outlook on the guitar. The book explores a variety of scales – major, minor, half-tone/whole-tone – and more.
00697237......................................$7.95

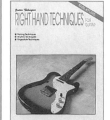

Right Hand Techniques

Through basic alternate, sweep and cross picking patterns, 10 chord arpeggios, palm muting and fingerstyle techniques, this book presents everything you need to know in getting started with the basic techniques needed to play every type of music. Additional topics include rhythm, rake and fingerstyle techniques. A real power packed technique book!
00699328......................................$6.95

Rock Chords For Guitar

Learn to play open-string, heavy metal power chords and bar chords with this book. This book introduces most of the chords needed to play today's rock 'n' roll. There are very clear fingering diagrams and chord frames on the top of each page. Empty staves at the bottom of each page allow the player to draw in his own chord patterns.
00689649 ....$6.95

Rock Scales For Guitar

This book contains all of the Rock, Blues, and Country scales employed in today's music. It shows the guitarist how scales are constructed and designed, how scales connect and relate to one another, how and where to use the scales they are learning, all of the possible scale forms for each different scale type, how to move each scale to new tonal areas and much, much more.
00699164 ....$6.95

Strums For Guitar

A handy guide that features 48 guitar strumming patterns for use with all styles of music. Also includes playing tips.
00699135 ....$6.95

FOR MORE INFORMATION, SEE YOUR LOCAL MUSIC DEALER,
OR WRITE TO:

HAL•LEONARD® CORPORATION

7777 W. BLUEMOUND RD. P.O. BOX 13819 MILWAUKEE, WI 53213

Prices, book contents & availability subject to change without notice.

0796

RECORDED VERSIONS GUITAR
RECORDED VERSIONS
The Best Note-For-Note Transcriptions Available

BOOKS INCLUDE TABLATURE

Adams, Bryan – Greatest Hits $19.95
Aerosmith – Greatest Hits $22.95
Aerosmith – Just Push Play $19.95
Alice in Chains – Acoustic $19.95
Alice in Chains – Dirt $19.95
Alice in Chains – Jar of Flies/Sap $19.95
Alice in Chains – Nothing Safe –
   The Best of the Box $19.95
Allman Brothers Band – Volume 1 . . . . . .$24.95
Allman Brothers Band – Volume 2 . . . . . .$24.95
Allman Brothers Band – Volume 3 . . . . . .$24.95
American Hi-Fi $19.95
Atkins, Chet – Vintage Fingerstyle $19.95
Audio Adrenaline, Best of $17.95
Bad Company Original Anthology - Bk 1 . .$19.95
Bad Company Original Anthology - Bk 2 . .$19.95
Beatles: 1962-1966 . . . .$24.95
Beatles: 1967-1970 . . . .$24.95
Beatles – Abbey Road $19.95
Beatles – Book 1 (White Album) $19.95
Beatles – For Acoustic Guitar $19.95
Beatles – Guitar Book $19.95
Beatles –
   Sgt. Pepper's Lonely Hearts Club Band . .$19.95
Beck – Midnite Vultures $19.95
Benson, George – Best of $19.95
Berry, Chuck $19.95
Black Sabbath –
   We Sold Our Soul for Rock 'N' Roll $19.95
Blink 182 – Dude Ranch $19.95
Blink 182 – Enema of the State $19.95
Blink 182 – Take Off Your Pants & Jacket .$19.95
Blue Oyster Cult – Cult Classics $19.95
Buchanan, Roy – Collection $19.95
Bowie, David – Best of $19.95
Buckley, Jeff – Collection $24.95
Cake – Songbook $19.95
Chapman, Steven Curtis – Best of $19.95
Cheap Trick – Best of $19.95
Chicago – Definitive Guitar Collection $22.95
Clapton Chronicles – Best of Eric Clapton .$18.95
Clapton, Eric – Selections from Blues $19.95
Clapton, Eric – The Cream of Clapton $24.95
Clapton, Eric – From the Cradle $19.95
Clapton, Eric – Journeyman $19.95
Clapton, Eric – Unplugged $22.95
Clapton, Eric/John Mayall – Bluesbreakers .$19.95
Clash, Best of $19.95
Coldplay – Parachutes $19.95
Counting Crows – August & Everything After .$19.95
Cream – Disraeli Gears $19.95
Creed – Human Clay $19.95
Creed – My Own Prison $19.95
dc Talk – Intermission: The Greatest Hits . .$19.95
Deep Purple, Best of $17.95
Di Franco, Ani – Best of $19.95
Di Franco, Ani – Little Plastic Castle $19.95
Di Franco, Ani – Up Up Up Up Up Up $19.95
Dire Straits – Sultans of Swing $19.95
Doors, The – Anthology $22.95
Doors, The – Essential Guitar Collection . .$16.95
Etheridge, Melissa – Skin $19.95
Eve 6 . . . .$19.95
Everclear, Best of $19.95
Extreme II – Pornograffitti $19.95
Fastball – All the Pain Money Can Buy $19.95
Foo Fighters – The Colour and the Shape .$19.95

00690394 Foo Fighters –
   There Is Nothing Left to Lose $19.95
00690222 G3 Live – Satriani, Vai, Johnson $22.95
00690536 Garbage – Beautiful Garbage $19.95
00690438 Genesis Guitar Anthology $19.95
00690338 Goo Goo Dolls – Dizzy Up the Girl $19.95
00690114 Guy, Buddy – Collection Vol. A-J $22.95
00690193 Guy, Buddy – Collection Vol. L-Y $22.95
00694798 Harrison, George – Anthology $19.95
00692930 Hendrix, Jimi – Are You Experienced? $24.95
00692931 Hendrix, Jimi – Axis: Bold As Love $22.95
00694944 Hendrix, Jimi – Blues $24.95
00692932 Hendrix, Jimi – Electric Ladyland $24.95
00690218 Hendrix, Jimi – First Rays of the New Rising Sun$27.95
00690017 Hendrix, Jimi – Woodstock $24.95
00660029 Holly, Buddy $19.95
00690054 Hootie & The Blowfish –
   Cracked Rear View $19.95
00690457 Incubus – Make Yourself $19.95
00690544 Incubus – Morningview $19.95
00690136 Indigo Girls – 1200 Curfews $22.95
00694833 Joel, Billy – For Guitar $19.95
00694912 Johnson, Eric – Ah Via Musicom $19.95
00694799 Johnson, Robert – At the Crossroads $19.95
00690271 Johnson, Robert – The New Transcriptions .$24.95
00699131 Joplin, Janis – Best of $19.95
00693185 Judas Priest – Vintage Hits $19.95
00690444 King, B.B. and Eric Clapton –
   Riding with the King $19.95
00690339 Kinks, The – Best of $19.95
00690279 Liebert, Ottmar + Luna Negra –
   Opium Highlights $19.95
00694755 Malmsteen, Yngwie – Rising Force $19.95
00694956 Marley, Bob – Legend $19.95
00694945 Marley, Bob – Songs of Freedom $24.95
00690283 McLachlan, Sarah – Best of $19.95
00690382 McLachlan, Sarah – Mirrorball $19.95
00690442 Matchbox 20 – Mad Season $19.95
00690239 Matchbox 20 – Yourself or Someone Like You .$19.95
00694952 Megadeth – Countdown to Extinction $19.95
00690391 Megadeth – Risk $19.95
00694951 Megadeth – Rust in Peace $22.95
00690495 Megadeth – The World Needs a Hero $19.95
00690040 Miller, Steve, Band – Greatest Hits $19.95
00690448 MxPx – The Ever Passing Moment $19.95
00690189 Nirvana – From the Muddy
   Banks of the Wishkah $19.95
00694913 Nirvana – In Utero $19.95
00694883 Nirvana – Nevermind $19.95
00690026 Nirvana – Unplugged™ in New York $19.95
00690121 Oasis – (What's the Story) Morning Glory .$19.95
00690358 Offspring, The – Americana $19.95
00690485 Offspring, The – Conspiracy of One $19.95
00690203 Offspring, The – Smash $18.95
00694847 Osbourne, Ozzy – Best of $22.95
00694830 Osbourne, Ozzy – No More Tears $19.95
00690538 Oysterhead – The Grand Pecking Order . .$19.95
00694855 Pearl Jam – Ten $19.95
00690439 Perfect Circle, A – Mer De Noms $19.95
00690176 Phish – Billy Breathes $22.95
00690424 Phish – Farmhouse $19.95
00690240 Phish – Hoist $19.95
00690331 Phish – Story of the Ghost $19.95
00690428 Pink Floyd – Dark Side of the Moon $19.95
00690456 P.O.D. – The Fundamental
   Elements of Southtown $19.95
00693864 Police, The – Best of $19.95

00690299 Presley, Elvis – Best of Elvis:
   The King of Rock 'n' Roll $19.95
00694975 Queen – Greatest Hits $24.95
00694910 Rage Against the Machine $19.95
00690395 Rage Against the Machine –
   The Battle of Los Angeles $19.95
00690145 Rage Against the Machine – Evil Empire . .$19.95
00690478 Rage Against the Machine – Renegades . . .$19.95
00690426 Ratt – Best of $19.95
00690055 Red Hot Chili Peppers –
   Bloodsugarsexmagik $19.95
00690379 Red Hot Chili Peppers – Californication . .$19.95
00690090 Red Hot Chili Peppers – One Hot Minute . .$22.95
00694899 R.E.M. – Automatic for the People $19.95
00690014 Rolling Stones – Exile on Main Street $24.95
00690135 Rush, Otis – Collection $19.95
00690502 Saliva – Every Six Seconds $19.95
00690031 Santana's Greatest Hits $19.95
00120123 Shepherd, Kenny Wayne – Trouble Is $19.95
00690419 Slipknot $19.95
00690530 Slipknot – Iowa $19.95
00690330 Social Distortion – Live at the Roxy $19.95
00690385 Sonicflood $19.95
00694957 Stewart, Rod – Unplugged...And Seated . .$22.95
00690021 Sting – Fields of Gold $19.95
00690519 Sum 41 – All Killer No Filler $19.95
00690425 System of a Down $19.95
00690531 System of a Down – Toxicity $19.95
00694824 Taylor, James – Best of $16.95
00690238 Third Eye Blind $19.95
00690403 Third Eye Blind – Blue $19.95
00690295 Tool – Aenima $19.95
00690039 Vai, Steve – Alien Love Secrets $24.95
00690343 Vai, Steve – Flex-able Leftovers $19.95
00660137 Vai, Steve – Passion & Warfare $24.95
00690392 Vai, Steve – The Ultra Zone $19.95
00690370 Vaughan, Stevie Ray and Double Trouble –
   The Real Deal: Greatest Hits Volume 2 . . .$22.95
00690455 Vaughan, Stevie Ray – Blues at Sunrise . . .$19.95
00690116 Vaughan, Stevie Ray – Guitar Collection . .$24.95
00660136 Vaughan, Stevie Ray – In Step $19.95
00660058 Vaughan, Stevie Ray –
   Lightnin' Blues 1983-1987 . . . .$24.95
00690417 Vaughan, Stevie Ray – Live at Carnegie Hall .$19.95
00694835 Vaughan, Stevie Ray – The Sky Is Crying . .$22.95
00690015 Vaughan, Stevie Ray – Texas Flood $19.95
00120026 Walsh, Joe – Look What I Did... . . . .$24.95
00694789 Waters, Muddy – Deep Blues $24.95
00690071 Weezer $19.95
00690516 Weezer (The Green Album) $19.95
00690286 Weezer – Pinkerton $19.95
00690447 Who, The – Best of $24.95
00690320 Williams, Dar – Best of $17.95
00690319 Wonder, Stevie – Some of the Best $17.95
00690443 Zappa, Frank – Hot Rats $19.95

EASY GUITAR
WITH NOTES & TAB

This series features simplified arrangement with notes, TAB, chord charts, and strum an pick patterns.

00702002	Acoustic Rock Hits	$12.95
00702001	Best of Aerosmith	$12.95
00702040	Best of Allman Brothers	$9.95
00702166	All-Time Best Guitar Collection	$16.95
00702169	Best of The Beach Boys	$10.95
00702143	Best Chart Hits	$8.95
00702066	Best Contemporary Hits	$9.95
00702140	Best of Brooks and Dunn	$10.95
00702095	Best of Mariah Carey	$10.95
00702043	Best of Johnny Cash	$12.95
00702033	Best of Steven Curtis Chapman	$12.95
00702073	Steven Curtis Chapman – Favorites	$10.95
00702115	Blues Classics	$10.95
00385020	Broadway Songs for Kids	$9.95
00702149	Christian Children's Songbook	$7.95
00702090	Eric Clapton's Best	$10.95
00702086	Eric Clapton from "Unplugged"	$10.95
00702016	Classic Blues	$12.95
00702141	Classic Rock	$8.95
00702053	Best of Patsy Cline	$10.95
00702170	Contemporary Christian Christmas	$9.95
00702006	Contemporary Christian Favorites	$9.95
00702091	Contemporary Country Ballads	$9.95
00702089	Contemporary Country Pickin'	$9.95
00702065	Contemporary Women of Country	$9.95
00702121	Country from the Heart	$9.95
00702145	Best of Jim Croce	$10.95
00702085	Disney Movie Hits	$9.95
00702122	The Doors	$10.95
00702041	Favorite Hymns	$9.95
00702068	Forty Songs for a Better World	$10.95
00702159	Best of Genesis	$10.95
00702174	God Bless America and Other Songs for a Better Nation	$8.95
00702057	Golden Age of Rock	$8.95
00699374	Gospel Favorites	$14.95
00702099	Best of Amy Grant	$9.95
00702113	Grease Is Still the Word	$9.95
00702160	Great American Country Songbook	$12.95
00702050	Great Classical Themes	$6.95
00702131	Great Country Hits of the '90s	$8.95
00702116	Greatest Hymns for Guitar	$7.95
00702130	The Groovy Years	$9.95
00702136	Best of Merle Haggard	$10.95
00702037	Hits of the '50s	$10.95
00702035	Hits of the '60s	$10.95
00702046	Hits of the '70s	$8.95
00702047	Hits of the '80s	$8.95
00702054	Best of Hootie and the Blowfish	$9.95
00702059	Hunchback of Notre Dame & Hercules	$9.95
00702032	International Songs	$12.95
00702045	Jailhouse Rock, Kansas City and Other Hits by Leiber & Stoller	$10.95

00702021	Jazz Standards	$14.95
00702051	Jock Rock	$9.95
00702087	New Best of Billy Joel	$10.95
00702088	New Best of Elton John	$9.95
00702162	Jumbo Easy Guitar Songbook	$19.95
00702011	Best of Carole King	$12.95
00702112	Latin Favorites	$9.95
00702097	John Lennon – Imagine	$9.95
00699003	Lion King & Pocahontas	$9.95
00702005	Best of Andrew Lloyd Webber	$12.95
00702061	Love Songs of the '50s & '60s	$9.95
00702062	Love Songs of the '70s & '80s	$9.95
00702063	Love Songs of the '90s	$9.95
00702129	Songs of Sarah McLachlan	$12.95
00702138	Mellow Rock Hits	$10.95
00702147	Motown's Greatest Hits	$9.95
00702112	Movie Love Songs	$9.95
00702039	Movie Themes	$10.95
00702117	My Heart Will Go On & Other Top Hits	$9.95
00702096	Best of Nirvana	$14.95
00702026	'90s Rock	$12.95
00702067	The Nutcracker Suite	$5.95
00699261	Oasis	$14.95
00702030	Best of Roy Orbison	$12.95
00702158	Songs from Passion	$9.95
00702125	Praise and Worship for Guitar	$9.95
00702139	Elvis Country Favorites	$9.95
00702038	Elvis Presley – Songs of Inspiration	$10.95
00702004	Rockin' Elvis	$9.95
00699415	Best of Queen	$12.95
00702155	Rock Hits for Guitar	$9.95
00702128	Rockin' Down the Highway	$8.95
00702135	Rock'n'Roll Romance	$9.95
00702092	Best of the Rolling Stones	$10.95
00702093	Rolling Stones Collection	$17.95
00702101	17 Chart Hits	$9.95
00702137	Solid Gold Rock	$9.95
00702110	The Sound of Music	$8.95
00702010	Best of Rod Stewart	$12.95
00702049	Best of George Strait	$10.95
00702042	Today's Christian Favorites	$8.95
00702124	Today's Christian Rock	$8.95
00702171	Top Chart Hits for Guitar	$8.95
00702029	Top Hits of '95-'96	$12.95
00702034	Top Hits of '96-'97	$12.95
00702007	TV Tunes for Guitar	$12.95
00702108	Best of Stevie Ray Vaughan	$10.95
00702123	Best of Hank Williams	$9.95
00702111	Stevie Wonder – Guitar Collection	$9.95

FOR MORE INFORMATION, SEE YOUR LOCAL MUSIC DEALER,
OR WRITE TO:

HAL•LEONARD®
CORPORATION

7777 W. BLUEMOUND RD. P.O. BOX 13819 MILWAUKEE, WI 53213

www.halleonard.com

Prices, contents and availability subject to change without notice.
Disney characters and artwork © Disney Enterprises, Inc.

0102

More Fingerstyle Favorites
from

Your Favorite Music For Guitar Made Easy

American Folksongs for Easy Guitar

Over 70 songs, including: All The Pretty Little Horses • Animal Fair • Aura Lee • Billy Boy • Buffalo Gals (Won't You Come Out Tonight) • Bury Me Not On The Lone Prairie • Camptown Races • (Oh, My Darling) Clementine • (I Wish I Was In) Dixie • The Drunken Sailor • Franky And Johnny • Home On The Range • Hush, Little Baby • I've Been Working On The Railroad • Jacob's Ladder • John Henry • My Old Kentucky Home • She'll Be Comin' Round The Mountain • Shenandoah • Simple Gifts • Swing Low, Sweet Chariot • The Wabash Cannon Ball • When Johnny Comes Marching Home • and more!
00702031 ....$12.95

The Big Christmas Collection

Includes over 70 Christmas favorites, such as: Ave Maria • Blue Christmas • Deck the Hall • Feliz Navidad • Frosty the Snow Man • Happy Holiday • A Holly Jolly Christmas • Joy to the World • O Holy Night • Silver and Gold • Suzy Snowflake • You're All I Want for Christmas • and more.
00698978....................................$16.95

The Broadway Book

93 unforgettable songs from 57 shows, including: Ain't Misbehavin' • Beauty and the Beast • Cabaret • Camelot • Don't Cry for Me Argentina • Edelweiss • Hello Dolly • I Whistle a Happy Tune • One • People • Sound of Music • Tomorrow • and more.
00702015 ...$17.95

The Big Book of Children's Songs

A comprehensive collection of 88 songs, including: Alphabet Song • Baa Baa Black Sheep • The Ballad of Davy Crockett • Beauty and the Beast • Bingo • The Brady Bunch • The Candy Man • Edelweiss • Everything Is Beautiful • (Meet) The Flintstones • I'm Popeye the Sailor Man • On Top of Spaghetti • Puff the Magic Dragon • Sailing Sailing • Supercalifragilisticexpialidocious • Twinkle, Twinkle Little Star • Yellow Submarine • and more.
00702027 ....$9.95

The Classic Country Book

Over 100 favorite country hits including Another Somebody Done Someboc Wrong Song • Could I Have This Danc • Don't It Make My Brown Eyes Blue • Elvi • Folsom Prison Blues • The Gambler Heartaches By The Number • I Fall 1 Pieces • Kiss An Angel Good Mornin' Lucille • The Most Beautiful Girl In The World • Oh, Lonesom Me • Rocky Top • Sixteen Tons • Tumbling Tumbleweeds • W The Circle Be Unbroken • You Needed Me • and more.
00702018....................................$19.95

The Classic Rock Book

89 monumental songs from the '60's, '70 and '80's, such as: American Woma • Born To Be Wild • Cocaine • Dust In Th Wind • Fly Like An Eagle • Gimme Thre Steps • I Can See For Miles • Lay • Magic Carpet Ride • Reelin' In The Yea • Sweet Home Alabama • Tumbling Dic • Walk This Way • You Really Got Me • and more.
00698977....................................$19.95

National Anthems For Easy Guitar

50 official national anthems in the original language, complete with stru and pick patterns and chord frame Countries represented include Australi Brazil, Canada, Cuba, France, German Great Britain, Haiti, Irish Republic, Mexic Peru, Poland, Russia, Sweden, Unite States of America, and more.
00702025 ....$12.95

The New Country Hits Book

100 hot country hits including: Ach Breaky Heart • Ain't Going Down ('Til Th Sun Comes Up) • Blame It On Your Hea • Boot Scootin' Boogie • Chattahooche • Don't Rock The Jukebox • Friends Low Places • Honky Tonk Attitude • I Fe Lucky • I Take My Chances • Little Les Talk And A Lot More Action • Mercury Blues • One More La Chance • Somewhere In My Broken Heart • T-R-O-U-B-L • The Whiskey Ain't Workin' • and more.
00702017....................................$19.95

FOR MORE INFORMATION, SEE YOUR LOCAL MUSIC DEALER, OR WRITE TO:

HAL•LEONARD®
CORPORATION
7777 W. BLUEMOUND RD. P.O. BOX 13819 MILWAUKEE, WI 53213

Contact Hal Leonard on the internet at http://www.halleonard.com